CogLab
on a CD

CogLab
on a CD

Greg Francis
Purdue University

Ian Neath
Memorial University

Daniel R. VanHorn
Purdue University

WADSWORTH
CENGAGE Learning

Australia • Brazil • Japan • Korea • Mexico • Singapore • Spain • United Kingdom • United States

WADSWORTH
CENGAGE Learning

ISBN-13: 978-0-495-09064-9
ISBN-10: 0-495-09064-6

Wadsworth
10 Davis Drive
Belmont, CA 94002-3098
USA

Cengage Learning is a leading provider of customized learning solutions with office locations around the globe, including Singapore, the United Kingdom, Australia, Mexico, Brazil, and Japan. Locate your local office at: **www.cengage.com/global**.

Cengage Learning products are represented in Canada by Nelson Education, Ltd.

To learn more about Wadsworth, visit **www.cengage.com/wadsworth**.

Purchase any of our products at your local college store or at our preferred online store **www.ichapters.com**.

6 7 12

CONTENTS

Introduction to CogLab

Welcome to the Cognitive Psychology Laboratory (CogLab™), a set of demonstrations of classic and current experiments and concepts from cognitive psychology. CogLab allows students to experience a variety of important experimental studies, which will help them understand the design of the study, the data, and the significance of the research.

CogLab On A CD is designed to work on computers running Microsoft Windows XP and MacOS X.

CogLab Demonstrations include:

Attention	Perception	Neurocognition
Attentional Blink	Apparent Motion	Brain Asymmetry
Change Detection	Garner Interference	Blind Spot
Simon Effect	Muller-Lyer Illusion	Receptive Fields
Spatial Cueing	Signal Detection	
Stroop Effect	Visual Search	
Sensory Memory	**Short-Term Memory**	**Working Memory**
Metacontrast Masking	Brown-Peterson	Irrelevant Speech Effect
Modality Effect	Position Error	Memory Span
Partial Report	Sternberg Search	Operation Span
Suffix Effect		Phonological Similarity Effect
Memory Process	**Metamemory**	**Imagery**
Encoding Specificity	False Memory	Link Word
Levels of Processing	Forgot-It-All-Along Effect	Mental Rotation
Serial Position	Remember/Know	
Von Restorff Effect		
Speech & Language	**Concepts**	**Judgment**
Categorical Perception – Identification	Absolute Identification	Monty Hall
Categorical Perception – Discrimination	Implicit Learning	Decision Making
Lexical Decision	Prototypes	Risky Decisions
Word Superiority		Typical Reasoning
		Wason Selection Task

Getting Started with CogLab

CogLab is a program that allows you to explore aspects of Cognitive Psychology by participating in various experiments. This version of CogLab is run off a CD. Start by inserting the CogLab CD into the CD drive of your computer. To start the CogLab program follow the instructions for your operating system, as discussed below.

Microsoft Windows XP

The CogLab program should start automatically. You will know the program is loading if you see the following:

Depending on the speed of your computer, it may take a few minutes for the program to load. If you don't see the picture shown above, you may need to start CogLab manually. Use the file explorer to look at the files on the CD. Double click on the file called *COGLAB.exe*.

CogLab on a CD should also work with older versions of Windows (back to 98SE) and on Windows Vista, but the program has not been fully tested on those systems.

MacOS X (10.2 or higher)

Use the Finder to show the contents of the CD. Double-click on the application called CogLab On A CD.jar (depending on your system settings, you may or may not see the ending .jar). On MacOS X, you will see the same start-up window shown above followed by the main window (next page).

4

The CogLab Main Window

When the program has finished loading and is running, you will see a window similar to the one below (shown as it appears on Windows XP). This is the main CogLab window. From this window you can start any experiment, or open saved CogLab data files. Each button on the main window corresponds to an experiment. Click once on the button for the experiment that you want to complete.

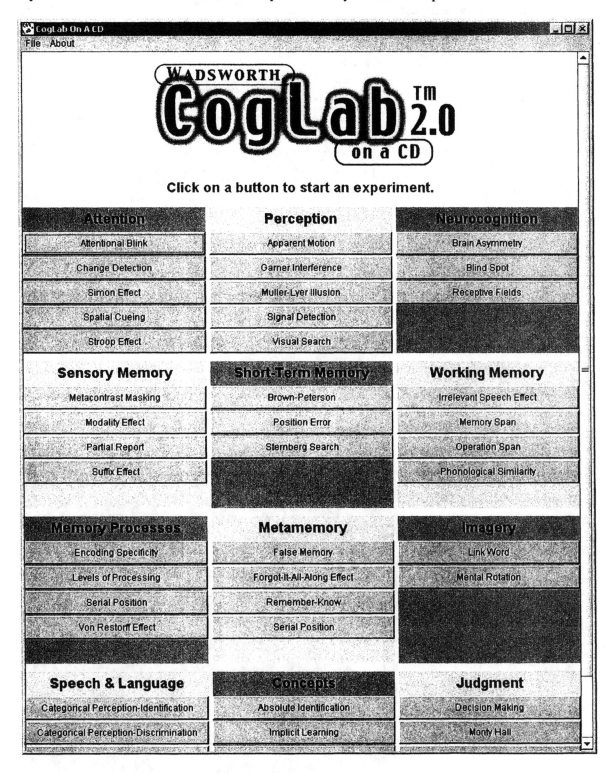

Running a CogLab Experiment

STEP 1: READ THE INTRODUCTION

After you click on an experiment button from the main CogLab window, a new window appears that displays the introduction for the experiment you want to run. Reading the introduction is very important, as it provides an explanation of what you should do during the experiment. Each experiment works differently.

STEP 2: ENTER YOUR NAME

At the bottom of the introduction window is a place for you to enter your first and last name. The names you enter will be included in the data that you generate. This embedding is useful if your instructor wants to verify that you completed assigned labs. After you enter your names, click on the *Do the experiment* button, or press the <return> key.

After you enter your names, an experiment window will appear. A smaller window will also appear with abbreviated instructions. Close the instructions window before starting the experiment. If necessary, you can open it again from the *CogLab Info.* menu. The graphic below shows the experiment window for a trial of the *Visual Search* demonstration. Each experiment looks different.

The *CogLab Info.* menu also has an item that shows how many trials remain in the experiment. As you proceed through the experiment, the trials to go will count down toward zero. You must complete all the trials in the experiment before you can see any results. If you stop the experiment before finishing, you will have to start over from the beginning.

6

STEP 3: SEE THE RESULTS

When you finish an experiment, the experiment window will close and shortly afterwards a summary of your data will appear. The graphic below shows typical results after completing the *Mental rotation* demonstration. The window has three tabs that show a brief explanation of the expected results and their significance, a tabular format of the data results and trial-by-trial data, and a plot of the data (if appropriate).

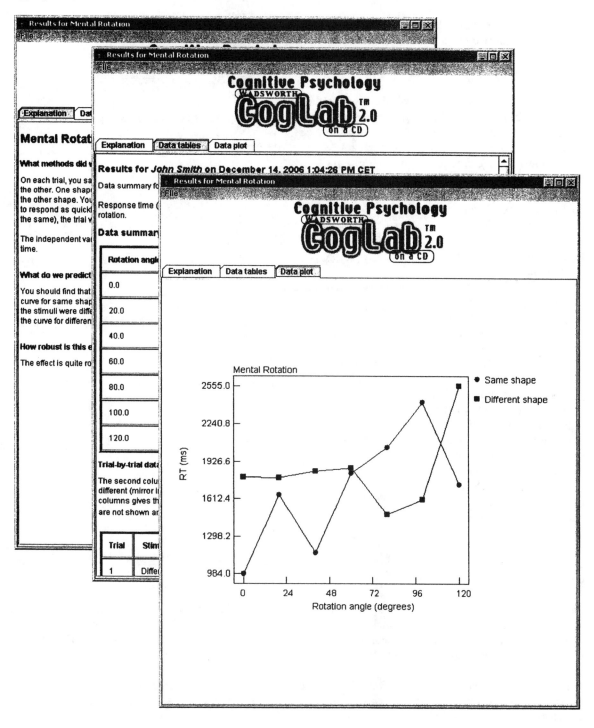

STEP 4: SAVE/PRINT THE RESULTS

After completing the experiment, you may want to print the results, import the data into a different program, or save the data for later analysis. Your instructor may also ask you to send him/her your saved data so that he/she can compile averages across your class.

The *File* menu on each results window provides methods for saving the data in two formats. By default the filename is always the name of the experiment appended to the name of the student, but this can be changed at the time of saving.

On Microsoft Windows XP, files will be saved to the My Documents folder by default, but you can also save the files to another folder with the file save window (right). Similar behavior holds for Mac OS.

CogLab can save data in two different formats. Which format is most appropriate depends on what you want to do with the data.

Save in CogLab format: This format preserves all the details of the CogLab results. The name you entered on step 2 is embedded in this format, along with the time that the experiment was finished. If your instructor wants you to send your results to him/her, this is probably the format he/she wants. Any file saved this way can be re-opened by CogLab using the *Open data in CogLab format* menu option under the *File* menu in the main CogLab window. This file will be saved with the extension *.cgl* so that it can be distinguished from other file types.

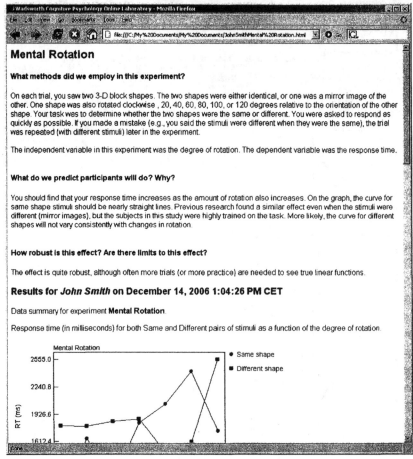

Save as HTML: This format converts all of the result summary window tabs into an html document that can be viewed by a variety of programs including web browsers, MS Word, and MS Excel. Use this format to incorporate your results into other documents. The graphic above shows the data for the *Mental rotation* experiment when it is saved as an HTML file and viewed in the Firefox web browser.

Printing: You can print the currently visible tab by selecting the *Print this page* item from the *File* menu of the results summary window. If you want all the data printed as a single file, save the data as an HTML document and print that file from a web browser.

STEP 5: ADDITIONAL ANALYSIS

CogLab data can be easily imported into other programs for additional analysis. Many programs, such as MS Word and MS Excel can read html files. If you saved your data as an html document, you can directly read in that file in to these programs.

You can also copy and paste text and tables of your from the result summary into these (and other) programs. To paste a data table or trial-by-trial data, highlight the text on the results summary window by selecting it with your mouse cursor. Copy the text using the keyboard shortcuts appropriate for your operating system (control-c or apple-c). Now go to the program in which you want to place the data table. Paste the text by using either the menu options (*Edit and Paste*) or the keyboard shortcuts appropriate for your operating system. If the program you paste into deals with tables of information, such as MS Excel, SPSS, or SigmaPlot, the data should appear with each cell of the table arranged appropriately for the program. The figure below shows the data table for the *False Memory* experiment as it appears after being pasted into MS Excel.

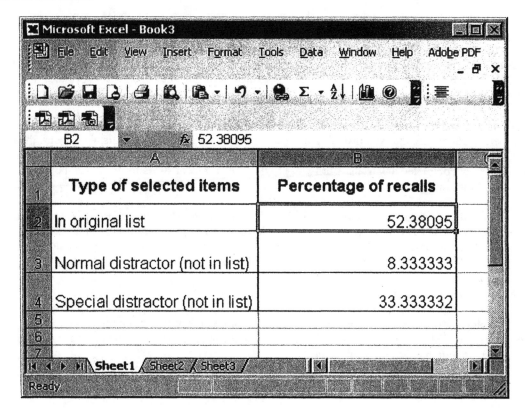

CogLab Help

Please see the *README.html* files on the CD for system specific information.

How much time does each experiment take?
Some experiments take only a few minutes whereas others can require nearly an hour. The introduction provides an estimate of the minimum time required to complete the experiment. You should allow an additional 5-10 minutes to read and understand the introduction and instructions, and an additional 5 minutes to contemplate the results. The estimated time does not include time for breaks.

Some experiments require a correct response on each trial. If you make many mistakes on one of these experiments, the experiment can take much longer.

Why doesn't the experiment begin?
If a window appears to start the experiment but nothing seems to happen, make certain that you are following the directions. Most experiments require you to press a key or click on a button to start an experimental trial. If the instructions ask you to press a key to start a trial, but nothing happens after the key press, click once in the middle of the window. Pressing the appropriate key should now produce a response from the window.

Why doesn't the "Trials to Go" menu item count down?
Some experiments require that you provide a correct answer on each trial. When mistakes occur, the trial is repeated later in the experiment. If you never answer correctly, the *Trials to go* menu label properly shows that you have not completed any trials. Until you provide the correct answers for the trials the experiment *will not* end. Make sure you read the instructions for that experiment.

I double-clicked on a data file saved in CogLab format, but CogLab didn't run; what happened?
Because *CogLab On A CD* is designed to be a cross-platform program, you cannot open a saved file by double-clicking on it. Instead, start the CogLab program and then select the *Open data in CogLab format* menu option under the *File* menu in the main CogLab window.

How do I get technical support?
If you purchased this CD new, you can obtain free technical support by going to http://psychology.wadsworth.com/CogLabCD/. Under the *About* menu item from the CogLab main window select the *Help* item for additional information on technical support. If you purchased this CD used, you are not eligible for technical support.

Experiments

Attentional Blink

Minimum time to complete this experiment: 30 minutes

Background

Cognitive mechanisms can handle only limited amounts of information. In many situations, there are more stimuli and mental events than resources for processing. As a result, some stimuli are processed and some are not. Selectively choosing some stimuli and ignoring others is called *attention*. Many studies of attention investigate how mental resources are switched from one stimulus to another. This experiment explores some properties of attention with rapidly changing stimuli. It shows that there is a brief time after paying attention to one stimulus when attention cannot be focused on a subsequent stimulus. This duration is called an *attentional blink* because it is analogous to being unable to see objects during an eye blink.

In the experiment, many letters are shown in rapid succession, with each letter overwriting the previous letter. The observer's task is to watch the entire sequence and then indicate whether certain target letters were in the sequence. The sequences are carefully constructed to systematically vary the temporal separation between two target letters. Thus, if the target letters are J and K, a sequence with the letters ". . . JXTVRK . . ." places K five letter-spaces beyond J.

The notable finding is that identification of the second target letter is very low when it quickly follows the first target letter. As temporal separation increases, identification of the second letter improves. This finding suggests that when the observer sees the first target letter, he/she must attend to it to ensure that it will be remembered later. The focusing of attention to that letter apparently requires time, and if the second target letter appears during that time, it is not attended and not reported. By looking at recognition of the second letter as a function of separation, we can estimate the time required to focus and break attention for stimuli.

Instructions

A window will fill the entire screen, and a smaller window will appear with abbreviated instructions. Close the instructions window. You can open it again later from the *CogLab Info.* menu.

Start a trial by pressing the *space* bar. A sequence of 19 letters will appear, with each new letter overwriting the previous one. Each letter is presented for only 100 milliseconds. After the letter sequence is finished, you will be prompted to make a response. Do not enter a response before the sequence is finished, or the trial will have to be discarded (and run again).

Your task is to determine whether the letter J and/or K were in the sequence of letters just presented. You indicate the presence of a J by pressing the *j* key and you indicate the presence of the K by pressing the *k* key. If you see both letters, press each in any order. If you did not see either letter, do not press either key. The screen will present the key you press, but this is only so you know the program received your key press; it is not feedback on whether you were correct. When you are ready for the next trial, press the *space* bar again.

If, for some reason, you need to discard a trial (e.g., you sneezed, your attention drifted, you "zoned out," et cetera), press the *t* key before pressing the *space* bar for the next trial. This will discard the just run trial. (It will be re-run later in the experiment.)

At the end of the experiment, the experiment window will close and a new window will appear that displays your data as a table and a plot (if appropriate) and provides an explanation of the experiment and results. You can print this information, save it as an html file, or save it in CogLab format. The latter format can be re-opened with CogLab on a CD and by your instructor who may want to combine data from students in your class.

Additional References

Dell'Acqua, R., Jolicoeur, P., Pesciarelli, F., Job, R., & Palomba, D. (2003). Electrophysiological evidence of visual encoding deficits in a cross-modal attentional blink paradigm. *Psychophysiology, 40*, 629-639.

Maki, W., Frigen, K., & Paulson, K. (1997). Associative priming by targets and distractors during rapid serial visual presentation: Does word meaning survive the attentional blink? *Journal of Experimental Psychology: Human Perception and Performance, 23*, 1014-1034.

Raymond, J., Shapiro, K., & Arnell, K. (1992). Temporary suppression of visual processing in an RSVP task: An attentional blink? *Journal of Experimental Psychology: Human Perception and Performance, 18*, 849-860.

Basic Questions

1. What is the main function of attention?

2. What does attentional blink tell us about attention?

3. Human behavior is often broken down into three stages: perception, cognition, and response execution. With what stage is attentional blink associated?

Advanced Questions

1. Use your personal data plot to calculate your attentional blink (in ms) for this activity.

2. What are some occupations in which a workers' performance could be adversely affected by attentional blink?

3. Using the occupations identified in question 2, what types of problems/mistakes might occur?

Discussion Question

1. In this demonstration, letters were used as targets. The target used can influence the duration of one's attentional blink. What other targets could have been used for this experiment? Predict the effects each of these targets would have on the duration of one's attentional blink as compared to the activity you recently completed. Explain the reasoning behind your predictions.

Change Detection

Minimum time to complete this experiment: 15 minutes

Background

The above picture shows a street in Vacouver, Canada, alternating with a light gray background. (The picture changes and so cannot be printed in this manual. Please go to CogLab on a CD to see this picture.) There are actually two different photographs of the road. Can you spot what is changing?

Chances are, you don't see anything changing right away, and it should take you a while to spot the change. Once you know what to look for, however, the change is obvious. (The answer is at the bottom of the page.)

The picture illustrates change blindness (Rensink, 2002) or, more accurately, how difficult it can be to detect change. The basic idea is that people do not store many details of a scene in memory. Rather, the critical factor seems to be attention: In order to see an object change, it is necessary to attend to the object.

The animated image illustrates Rensink's *flicker paradigm* in which an original image is followed by a blank image (a mask) and is then followed by a changed image (and another mask). The blank image swamps the local-motion signal that would ordinarily be caused by a change in an object, so attention is not drawn to the change. The presence of the mask prevents automatic detection of change. Change must now be detected by a slower, higher-level process. Basically, you have to search the scene, object by object until you happen to find the changed object.

Instructions

A window will appear that fills nearly the entire screen, and a smaller window will appear with abbreviated instructions. Close the instructions window. You can open it again later from the *CogLab Info.* menu.

Press the space bar key to start a trial. You will see a message that the images are being loaded. This may take a few seconds. You will then see two pictures alternating. Text on the far right will indicate which image (Image 1 or Image 2) is being shown. Sometimes, the pictures will be separated by a gray field; sometimes they won't. Your task is to decide if anything is changing between the two versions of the picture. If something is changing, press the *c* key. If nothing is changing, press the *n* key. You should try to respond as quickly and as accurately as you can.

There are 16 trials, half with a change and half without a change, and half with flicker (the gray field) and half without.

At the end of the experiment, the experiment window will close and a new window will appear that displays your data as a table and a plot (if appropriate) and provides an explanation of the experiment and results. You can print this information, save it as an html file, or save it in CogLab format. The latter format can be re-opened with CogLab on a CD and by your instructor who may want to combine data from students in your class.

In the picture at the top of the page, a light from a lamp post disappears.

Additional References

Eimer, M., & Mazza, V. (2005). Electrophysiological correlates of change detection. *Psychophysiology, 42*, 328-342.

Cole, G., Kentridge, R., Gellatly, A., & Heywood, C. (2003). Detectability of onsets versus offsets in the change detection paradigm. *Journal of Vision, 3*, 22-31.

Simons, D. (2000). Current approaches to change blindness. *Visual Cognition, 7*, 1-15.

Basic Questions

1. Was it harder for you to detect a scene change in the trials with or without a flicker between photographs? Does your data support your evaluation? Explain.

2. What effect does the flicker have on attention?

3. What type of search strategy is commonly used in the no-flicker condition? What type of search strategy is commonly used in the flicker condition?

Advanced Questions

1. Why is reaction-time reported with your experimental results, instead of just reporting your percent correct?

2. Which condition of the demonstration is equivalent to the following driving situations: looking down to turn the radio station, picking up your cell phone, or checking your speedometer? What types of problems can arise from these behaviors?

3. The flash used in the flicker condition is also used to divert or attract your attention in many experiences you have probably had. Describe an experience you have had that utilized a flash. What was the effect of the flash?

Discussion Question

1. Identify and describe at least two factors that will determine one's ability to detect a change in a scene?

Simon Effect

Minimum time to complete this experiment: 15 minutes

Background

The Simon effect refers to the finding that people are faster and more accurate when responding to stimuli that occur in the same relative location as the response, even though the location information is irrelevant to the actual task (Simon, 1969). Studying the Simon effect gives us insight into a stage of decision making called "response selection." According to information-processing theory, there are three stages of decision making: stimulus identification, response selection, and response execution or the motor stage.

Superficially, the Simon effect may seem similar to the Stroop effect. However, it is generally accepted that the interference that occurs in the Stroop effect comes from the stimulus identification stage, while the interference that occurs in the Simon effect occurs in the response-selection stage. During response selection, a person uses a rule to translate the relevant stimulus dimension, usually shape or color, to the correct left or right response. However, the location dimension of the stimulus (its position on the screen) overlaps with the relevant stimulus dimension (left or right). Because of this, the irrelevant location dimension of the stimulus activates the corresponding response and interferes with making a response to the non-corresponding side. As a result, same-side responses are faster and more accurate than opposite-side responses.

In the real world, the Simon effect has important implications. Primarily, it shows that location information cannot be ignored and will affect decision making, even if the user knows that the information is irrelevant. The Simon effect (and related phenomena) must be taken into account in design of man-machine interfaces. Good interfaces display information in ways that match the types of responses people should make. For example, imagine that you are flying a plane, and the left engine has a problem. The indicator for that engine should be to the left of a corresponding indicator for the right engine. If it is the other way around, you may respond incorrectly to the indicator and adjust the wrong engine. That could be problematic.

Instructions

A window will appear that fills nearly the entire screen, and a smaller window will appear with abbreviated instructions. Close the instructions window. You can open it again later from the *CogLab Info.* menu.

Position your hands so the index finger of your left hand is on the *v* key and the index finger of your right hand is on the *m* key. Press the space bar to start a trial. A fixation dot will appear in the middle of the window. Stare at it. A short time later (less than a second), you will be shown a red or green square to the left or right of fixation dot. Your task is to press the *v* key if the square is green and to press the *m* key if the square is red.

After each trial, you will be given feedback about whether your response was correct or incorrect, and how fast your reaction time was in milliseconds. If you respond before the stimulus appears or too long after the stimulus appears, you will be prompted to slow down or speed up.

There are at least 100 trials. If you make a mistake (e.g., report a green square as red), the trial will be repeated later in the experiment. You can discard a trial by pressing the *t* key instead of *v* or *m*. Discarding is appropriate if, after starting a trial, you sneeze, zone out, or are otherwise distracted. Discarded trials will be repeated later.

At the end of the experiment, the experiment window will close and a new window will appear that displays your data as a table and a plot (if appropriate) and provides an explanation of the experiment and results. You can print this information, save it as an html file, or save it in CogLab format. The latter format can be re-opened with CogLab on a CD and by your instructor who may want to combine data from students in your class.

Additional Resources

Urcuioli, P., Vu, K., & Proctor, R. (2005) A Simon Effect in Pigeons. *Journal of Experimental Psychology: General, 134*, 93-107.

Van der Lubbe, R., & Verleger, R. (2002). Aging and the Simon task. *Psychophysiology, 39*, 100-110.

Proctor, R., & Lu, C. (1999). Processing irrelevant location information: Practice and transfer effects in choice-reaction tasks. *Memory & Cognition, 27*, 63-77.

Basic Questions

1. The Simon Effect is the result of a conflict between two sources of information. Describe this conflict.

2. According to human information-processing theory, at what stage does the Simon Effect occur?

3. Look at your data. Did you show a Simon Effect? Explain how you know.

Advanced Questions

1. Consider the stove design below, using your knowledge about the Simon Effect. Identify a positive aspect of the design as well as an aspect with the design that could be problematic. (The knob on the far left corresponds to the stove coil on the bottom left, the knob second from the left corresponds to the stove coil on the top left, the knob second from the right corresponds to the stove coil on the top right, and the knob on the far right corresponds to the stove coil on the bottom right.)

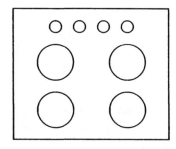

2. While you are driving, a pedestrian walks in front of your car from the right side and you do not have time to stop. Thinking only in terms of the Simon Effect, what would be your best course of action? Explain.

3. Many designs that utilize what is known about stimulus location and response compatibility (the Simon Effect) are evident in transportation. Think about the last few times you have been in a car and identify two of them.

Discussion Question

1. In this demonstration, you were shown targets to the left and right of your eye fixation and had to make a right or a left key press depending on the target. Describe another experimental setup in which you might find a Simon Effect. Be sure to identify the targets, responses, target locations, and the conflict that would cause the Simon Effect.

Spatial Cueing

Minimum time to complete this experiment: 20 minutes

Background

A "spotlight" is a metaphor that nicely captures many characteristics of the focus of visual attention: It is a "beam" that is moved spatially, that may not be divided, and that enhances the detection of events falling within it.

Some of the strongest evidence supporting the unitary concept of attention comes from the luminance-detection paradigm (e.g., Posner, 1980). In such experiments, subjects are first cued with the likely spatial location of a target and then respond as rapidly as possible when the target appears at any location in the display. For example, in a typical display, the stimuli are arranged horizontally with a fixation point in the center, which is also the location where the cue appears. The cue is either valid, correctly identifying the spatial location of the target, or invalid, incorrectly identifying the location of the target. Following the presentation of the cue, a single target stimulus is illuminated (usually about 1000 ms after the onset of the cue) and subjects respond as soon as they detect the target, regardless of its location. Relative to a neutral cue condition, responses are faster when the target appears in the cued location (a valid trial) and slower when the target appears in a non-cued location (an invalid trial).

Demonstrations of these patterns of results occur independently of eye movements. In other words, when an eye tracker verifies that your eyes are still fixed on the center, your focus of attention can be off to the right, or off to the left. While other interpretations of these findings are possible, they are consistent with the notion of a focused beam of attention that may be moved to distinct spatial locations - incorrectly in the case of an invalid trial and correctly in the case of a valid trial.

Instructions

A window will appear that fills nearly the entire screen, and a smaller window will appear with abbreviated instructions. Close the instructions window. You can open it again later from the *CogLab Info.* menu.

Start a trial by pressing the space bar. A fixation dot will appear in the middle of the window. Stare at it. A short time later, a cue will appear. If the arrow points to the right, 80% of the time the target will appear on the right. If the arrow points to the left, 80% of the time, the target will appear on the left. If no arrow appears, the target is equally likely to appear on the left or right. A short time after the cue disappears, a red square will appear.

Your task is to respond as quickly as possible when you see the square appear, regardless of its location. To respond, press the *n* key.

After pressing the *n* key, press the *space* bar to start the next trial. There are at least 80 trials. If you respond too soon or too late, the trial will be discarded and will be repeated later in the experiment.

At the end of the experiment, the experiment window will close and a new window will appear that displays your data as a table and a plot (if appropriate) and provides an explanation of the experiment and results. You can print this information, save it as an html file, or save it in CogLab format. The latter format can be re-opened with CogLab on a CD and by your instructor who may want to combine data from students in your class.

Additional Resources

Richards, J. (2005). Localizing cortical sources of event-related potentials in infants' covert orienting. *Developmental Science, 8*, 255-278.

Golla, H., Ignashchenkova, A., Haarmeier, T., & Thier, P. (2004). Improvement of visual acuity by spatial cueing: A comparative study in human and non-human primates. *Vision Research, 44*, 1589-1600.

Theeuwes, J. (1989). Effects of location and form cueing on the allocation of attention in the visual field. *Acta Psychologica, 72*, 177-192.

Basic Questions

1. Does visual attention always follow a person's eye movements? Explain.

2. What was the independent variable in this demonstration? What was the dependent variable?

3. In this demonstration, the cue arrows are examples of an endogenous cue. What is an endogenous cue? What is an exogenous cue?

Advanced Questions

1. In soccer, goalies find themselves in a difficult position during a penalty kick. In this situation, they often observe the opposing player as he/she approaches the ball to try and find an indicator of the direction the ball might go. Why would a goalie take this strategy and what are its implications?

2. Name a profession (other than a professional soccer player) in which an individual might give an invalid spatial cue. Why do they use these invalid cues?

3. Envision an experiment similar to the one you just completed in which you have to make a response in relation to the location of a target. In this experiment you are given either a blue or a red square as a target. Furthermore, instead of being given a location

cue you are given a cue about the color of the upcoming target. Do you think your valid-cue condition reaction-times would increase, decrease, or stay the same as compared to an uncued condition?

Discussion Question

1. In this demonstration, the arrow predicted the location of the target with 80% accuracy. What do you think the results would have looked like had the arrow predicted the target location with 50% accuracy? What about with 20% accuracy?

Stroop Effect

Minimum time to complete this experiment: 20 minutes

Background

When you first learned to tie your shoelaces, you needed to think carefully through each step of the process. Now, you probably do not even think about the steps, but simply initiate a series of movements that proceed without any further influence. When a behavior or skill no longer requires direct interaction, cognitive psychologists say it is *automatized.*

Many behaviors can become automatized: typing, reading, writing, bicycling, piano playing, driving, etc. Automatization is interesting because it is an important part of daily life. We perform a variety of automatized behaviors quickly and effortlessly. In some cases, people report that they do not consciously know *how* the behavior is performed, they just will it to happen and it does happen.

To explore properties of automatized behaviors, cognitive psychologists often put observers in a situation where an automatized response is in conflict with the desired behavior. This allows researchers to test the behind-the-scenes properties of automatized behaviors by noting their influence on more easily measured behaviors. This demonstration explores a well-known example of this type of influence, the Stroop effect.

Stroop (1935) noted that observers were slower to properly identify the color of ink when the ink was used to produce color names different from the color of the ink. That is, observers were slower to identify red ink when it spelled the word *blue.* This is an interesting finding because observers are told to not pay any attention to the word names and simply to report the color of the ink. However, this seems to be a nearly impossible task, as the name of the word seems to interfere with the observer's ability to report the color of the ink.

A common explanation for the Stroop effect is that observers (especially college undergraduates) have automatized the process of reading. Thus, the color names of the words are always processed very quickly, regardless of the color of the ink. On the other hand, identifying colors is not a task that observers have to report on very often and, because it is not automatized, it is slower. The fast and automatic processing of the color name of the word interferes with the reporting of the ink color.

Instructions

A window will appear that fills nearly the entire screen, and a smaller window will appear with abbreviated instructions. Close the instructions window. You can open it again later from the 'CogLab Info.' menu.

Start a trial by pressing the *space* bar. A fixation dot will appear in the middle of the window, stare at it. A short time later (less than a second) a word (RED, GREEN, or BLUE) will appear on the screen, and the word will be displayed in a red, green, or blue color. Your task is to classify, as quickly as possible, the font color, regardless of the word name. If the font color is red, press the *h* key; for green, press the *j* key; for blue, press the *k* key. It may take a bit of practice to remember which key corresponds to which font color.

After pressing a key to identify the font color, you will receive feedback on whether you were correct. If you were incorrect, the trial will be repeated later in the experiment. If you find you are making lots of mistakes, you should slow down or make certain you understood which key goes with which font color. Press the *space* bar to start the next trial.

There are at least 45 trials, 30 in which the font colors and word names are different, and 15 in which the font colors and color names match (e.g., the word RED in red font color). You can also discard a trial by pressing the *t* key instead of identifying the font color. Discarding is appropriate if, after starting a trial, you sneeze, zone out, or are otherwise distracted. Discarded trials will be repeated later.

At the end of the experiment, the experiment window will close and a new window will appear that displays your data as a table and a plot (if appropriate) and provides an explanation of the experiment and results. You can print this information, save it as an html file, or save it in CogLab format. The latter format can be re-opened with CogLab on a CD and by your instructor who may want to combine data from students in your class.

Additional Resources

Henik, A. & Salo, R. (2004). Schizophrenia and the Stroop Effect. *Behavioral and Cognitive Neuroscience Reviews, 3*, 42-59

Durgin, F. (2000). The reverse Stroop effect. *Psychonomic Bulletin & Review, 7*, 121-125.

Green, E. & Barber, P. (1981). An auditory Stroop effect with judgments of speaker gender. *Perception & Psychophysics, 30*, 459-466.

Basic Questions

1. Look at your individual data. Were you faster on congruent trials or incongruent trials? Does this surprise you? Why or why not?

2. What is the most commonly accepted explanation of why most people are slower on incongruent trials than on congruent trials in the Stroop task?

3. Imagine that in this demonstration you were asked to read the color words and to ignore the ink color in which the words are written. Using the explanation of the Stroop Effect given in the text, do you think your reaction-times on the incongruent trials would be faster, slower, or similar to the congruent trials?

Advanced Questions

1. What strategy could one use to overcome the Stroop Effect observed in this demonstration?

2. Name three tasks that are automatic for most people.

3. The data for this demonstration displays mean reaction-times and mean standard deviations. Usually subjects have a greater standard deviation on the incongruent trials than on the congruent trials. Why do you think this might be?

4. At a cross walk, there is often a signal that tells pedestrians when to walk and when not to walk. Typically these signals use an upright hand to represent do not walk and a human figure to indicate when walking is permitted. What colors are usually associated with these symbols? Do the colors and symbols seem congruent (support a correct response) or incongruent (inhibit a correct response)? Explain.

Discussion Question

1. What types of effects would you predict if a subject were given extensive training in a Stroop task before being tested? Why?

Apparent Motion

Minimum time to complete this experiment: 15 minutes

Background

If two stimuli are briefly flashed in rapid succession, observers will sometimes report seeing motion between the two stimuli. Reports of this type of apparent motion were investigated near the beginning of the 20th century by Gestalt psychologists (most notably Wertheimer). They noticed, among other things, that the timing of the flashes was important in determining whether or not motion was seen. If the time between the offset of the first stimulus and the onset of the second stimulus (called the interstimulus interval or ISI) is very short, observers simply see two dots presented nearly simultaneously. If the ISI is very long, observers see one dot flash on and off and then the other flash on and off. For intermediate ISIs, the first dot seems to turn off, move through the space between the dots, and appear at the position of the second dot.

Korte (1915) noted that the ISI thresholds for seeing motion versus being too short varied with the spatial separation of the stimuli. The farther apart the stimuli were, the longer the ISI needed to be for a good motion percept. This finding, and others, were formulated in a set of "Korte's laws" that have been used to describe aspects of apparent motion.

Instructions

A window will fill the entire screen, and a smaller window will appear with abbreviated instructions. Close the instructions window. You can open it again later from the *CogLab Info.* menu.

Press the *space* bar key to start a trial. After pressing the *space* bar, a small fixation square will appear in the middle of the screen. Stare at this square. It will disappear after one and a half seconds. Less than a second later, a dot will appear on the right and disappear, and then a dot will appear on the left and disappear. These stimuli will then cycle back and forth repeatedly. Each of the dots is presented for 150 milliseconds. The duration of the blank between dots (the ISI) is variable.

Your task is to adjust the ISI until the motion percept is as strong as you can make it. You can increase the ISI by 20 milliseconds by pressing the *i* key. You can decrease the ISI by 20 milliseconds by pressing the *k* key. The ISI can never become negative.

After you are satisfied that the motion percept is as strong as you can make it, press the *space* bar to start the next trial. The spacing of the dots will vary from trial to trial. There are five spacings and five replications for each spacing for a total of 25 trials.

At the end of the experiment, the experiment window will close and a new window will appear that displays your data as a table and a plot (if appropriate) and provides an explanation of the experiment and results. You can print this information, save it as an html file, or save it in CogLab format. The latter format can be re-opened with CogLab on a CD and by your instructor who may want to combine data from students in your class.

Additional References

Muckli, L., Kiregeskorte, N., Lanfermann, H., Zanella, F., Singer, W., & Goebel, R. (2002). Apparent motion: Event-related functional magnetic resonance imaging of perceptual switches and states. *Journal of Neuroscience, 22*, 3342-3444.

Koriat, A. (1994). Object-based apparent motion. *Perception & Psychophysics, 56*, 392-404.

Anstis, S., Giaschi, D., & Cogan, A. (1985). Adaptation to apparent motion. *Vision Research, 25*, 1051-1062.

Basic Questions

1. What is an ISI? How does it relate to apparent motion?

2. Using your personal data, which dot distance did you assign the shortest ISI? Which distance did you assign the longest ISI? Describe the relationships between the dot distances and the ISIs you assigned (linear, exponential, logarithmic, etc.).

3. What does one experience when an ISI is too slow? What does one experience when an ISI is too fast?

Advanced Questions

1. Using your personal data, what would you predict your optimal ISI to be if the flashing dots had a distance from the center of .40?

2. Name two things that use apparent motion that are not already mentioned in the text.

3. Apparent motion is dependent on factors other than ISI. Describe the various factors that would affect one's ability to perceive apparent motion. For each factor you identify, describe a situation in which it would facilitate apparent motion perception and one in which it would impair apparent motion perception.

Discussion Question

1. Describe some of the properties and/or limitations of the visual system that are consistent with the finding that apparent motion is often perceived in the same way as real motion.

Garner Interference

Minimum time to complete this experiment: 25 minutes

Background

In many perceptual tasks, people are asked to judge a stimulus on one dimension. For example, they might be asked to indicate whether the stimulus is light or dark (varies in terms of brightness). We can measure how quickly and accurately people make these decisions.

Sometimes, people are asked to make a decision, but the stimulus also varies along a second dimension. For example, the subject might be asked to judge the brightness of the stimulus (light or dark), but the stimulus might also vary in size. The size of the stimulus is irrelevant, only the brightness matters. In this type of situation, researchers are interested in whether the variation along the irrelevant dimension causes interference (*i.e.*, a decrease in speed of responding and accuracy).

According to Garner (1974), some dimensions are separable (*i.e.*, no interference), whereas others are integral (*i.e.*, there is interference). As the names suggest, people seem capable of processing two separable dimensions as two dimensions; however, people seem to process two integral dimensions as one dimension, hence the interference.

In the experiment below, you are asked to judge either the brightness (light or dark) or size (big or small) of a stimulus. In addition, the stimulus sometimes varies in saturation (how colorful the stimulus is, relative to plain gray). The computer will measure the time needed for you to make the judgment. Try to be as fast as possible, but do not go so fast that you make a lot of mistakes.

The experiment is broken in to several parts. In some parts, referred to later as a *baseline* condition, the stimulus is only one saturation, either high or low (the stimulus looks less or more gray). In other parts, called the *correlated* conditions, the stimulus can have high or low saturation. How it varies always matches with your task (to judge either the brightness or size of the stimulus). Thus, a high saturated stimulus might always be small and a low saturated stimulus might always be large. In the last condition, called the *filtering* condition, the stimulus varies in saturation, but can be paired with either other trait of the stimulus.

If the relevant and irrelevant stimulus dimensions are *separable*, then the visual system represents them independently. As a result, it will be fairly easy to focus your attention on just the dimension that matters for the judgment. The saturation of the stimulus should not interfere. The reaction time and percentage of correct judgments should not vary much across the different conditions.

On the other hand, if the relevant and irrelevant stimulus dimensions are *integral*, then the visual system represents them together. As a result, it will be difficult to focus your attention on just the dimension that matters for the judgment. In the version of the experiment with integral dimensions, the time needed to make the judgment (and possibly the accuracy of the judgment) will depend on the condition of the experiment. The reaction time should be shortest (and accuracy highest) for the correlated condition. In this condition, you could pay attention to either dimension and know how to respond. The reaction time might be a bit longer for the baseline condition because only the relevant dimension gives you the information you need. The other dimension does not help or hurt because it is always the same.

The slowest reaction time (and poorest percentage correct) should be found for the filtering condition. Here, both dimensions are randomly paired together. Because the dimensions are integrally related, it is difficult to focus on one and ignore the other. This should make the task more difficult and lead to a longer reaction time (or poorer percentage correct). The increase in reaction time for the filtering condition relative to the baseline condition is called *Garner interference*.

Instructions

A window will appear that fills nearly the entire screen, and a smaller window will appear with abbreviated instructions.

You will be randomly assigned to either the integral or separable version of the experiment. A window will appear that fills nearly the entire screen, and a smaller window will appear with abbreviated instructions. Read these instructions carefully, because they vary depending on which version of the experiment you are assigned. Close the instructions window. You can open it again later from the *CogLab Info.* menu.

Click on the space bar to start a trial. A reminder of which keys to press will appear at the top of the window. This is always the same. Less than a second later, the target stimulus will appear. Depending on the version of the experiment, your task is to judge either the size or brightness of the stimulus.

You want to respond as fast as possible, so keep your fingers over the response keys. After you respond, you will be given feedback on whether your judged correctly or incorrectly. If you find you are making many mistakes, you should slow down.

At the end of the experiment, the experiment window will close and a new window will appear that displays your data as a table and a plot (if appropriate) and provides an explanation of the experiment and results. You can print this information, save it as an html file, or save it in CogLab format. The latter format can be re-opened with CogLab on a CD and by your instructor who may want to combine data from students in your class.

Additional References

Patching, G., & Quinlan, P. (2002). Garner and congruence effects in the speeded classification of bimodal signals. *Journal of Experimental Psychology: Human Perception and Performance, 28,* 755-775.

Huettel, S., & Lockhead, G. (1999). Range effects of an irrelevant dimension on classification. *Perception & Psychophysics, 61,* 1624-1645.

Melara, R. (1989). Dimensional interaction between color and pitch. *Journal of Experimental Psychology: Human Perception and Performance, 15,* 69-79.

Basic Questions

1. Which version of the experiment did you complete (integral, separable)? Did you find some trials were more difficult than others?

2. Look at your data. Using what you know about Garner Interference, does your data follow the predicted pattern (keep in mind the version of the experiment you completed)? Explain your answer.

3. According to the ideas presented on Garner Interference, what determines whether two stimulus dimensions are integral or separable?

Advanced Questions

1. Using your trial-by-trial data, compute your standard deviation for the baseline and filtering conditions.

2. Consider your data, does the proportion-of-correct measure seem to support or contradict the reaction-time measure for each of the experimental conditions? Why or why not?

3. You are planning on painting your living room, so you go to the local hardware store to buy some paint. You want a color that gives you a perception of a specific kind of blue. The sales clerk lets you brush some of the paint you are interested in on an available piece of drywall. The color matches exactly what you had in mind. Can you now purchase the paint with confidence? Why or why not?

Discussion Question

1. What can the typical findings with Garner Interference tell us about people's perceptual judgments? Explain.

Muller-Lyer Illusion

Minimum time to complete this experiment: 25 minutes

Background

This experiment serves two purposes. First, it introduces a well-known perceptual illusion called the Muller-Lyer illusion. Second, it demonstrates a psychophysical experimental method called the method of constant stimuli.

The Muller-Lyer illusion is easily demonstrated. In the figure below, there are three horizontal lines. Two of the lines contain a pair of "wings." The wings are drawn outward or inward from the line ends. The illusion is that the line with the outward-drawn wings tends to look longer than the line with the inward-drawn wings. The line without wings tends to look smaller than the line with outward-drawn wings and bigger than the line with inward-drawn wings. It is an illusion because the lines are actually all the same length, which you can verify with a ruler.

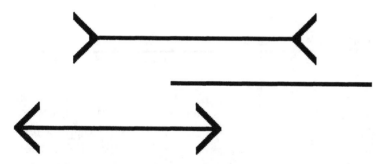

This experiment is not directly about experiencing the illusion, which can be done just by looking at the figure, but is about using the illusion to demonstrate a common experimental technique: the method of constant stimuli.

It is fun to look at visual illusions and realize how our perception differs from reality. To guide the development of theories on cognition and perception, however, we need more-specific data. We need to know, for example, just how long does the line with the wings drawn outward look? The more general question is, "How do we measure characteristics of percepts?" We cannot measure them directly because a perception is a particularly subjective experience.

The field of psychophysics deals with precisely this question. It attempts to relate reported characteristics of perception to physical properties. Instead of just asking an observer to look at and comment on stimuli, specific judgments are required and the stimuli are systematically varied. For the Muller-Lyer illusion, we will have observers compare the perception produced by a line with outward-drawn wings to the perception produced by lines with no wings. We will systematically vary the length of the line without wings to see when the perceived line lengths match. We can then look at the physical length of the matching line without wings and use that as a measure of the strength of the Muller-Lyer illusion. There are several ways to go about making such comparisons. One of the simplest and most powerful is the method of constant stimuli. We will generate a large set of lines without wings of varying lengths and have the observer compare each one with a standard line with wings. For each comparison the observer notes whether the line without wings is perceived to be bigger or smaller than the line with wings. Unlike some other psychophysical methods (like the method of adjustment), the stimuli are not changeable by the observer, thus they are constant stimuli. The observer's task is just to report on the perception.

The goal of this type of experiment is to produce a psychometric function, that is, a set of values that describes the probability of a certain response as a physical characteristic is varied. For the Muller-Lyer experiments, we will find the proportion of reports where the line without wings seemed bigger than the standard as a function of the physical length of the line without wings. With such a curve, you can often identify critical values, such as the point of subjective equality, where the line without wings seemed to be the same size as the line with wings (e.g., 50% of the time it is described as bigger and 50% of the time is described as smaller).

Instructions

A window will appear that fills nearly the entire screen, and a smaller window will appear with abbreviated instructions. Close the instructions window. You can open it again later from the *CogLab Info.* menu.

Press the space bar key to start a trial. After pressing the space bar, two vertical lines will appear. The line on the lower right has outward-drawn wings. The line on the upper left has no wings. Your task is to choose which vertical line is longer. Press the *z* key if the line on the left seems longer. Press the */* key if the vertical line on the right appears longer. A box will be drawn around your selection. You can change your response if you wish. When you are satisfied with your response, press the space bar key to start the next trial.

There are a total of 150 trials. Each trial only takes a few seconds to complete. Do not go too fast, though, or the computer will tell you to slow down and take time to make an accurate judgment of relative line lengths.

At the end of the experiment, the experiment window will close and a new window will appear that displays your data as a table and a plot (if appropriate) and provides an explanation of the experiment and results. You can print this information, save it as an html file, or save it in CogLab format. The latter format can be re-opened with CogLab on a CD and by your instructor who may want to combine data from students in your class.

Additional References

Predebon, J. (2005). A comparison of length-matching and length-fractionation measures of Muller-Lyer distortions. *Perception & Psychophysics, 67,* 264-273.

Welch, R., Post, R., Lum, W., & Prinzmetal, W. (2004). The relationship between perceived length and egocentric location in Muller-Lyer figures with one versus two chevrons. *Perception & Psychophysics, 66*, 1095-1104.

Morikawa, K. (2003). An application of the Muller-Lyer illusion. *Perception, 32*, 121-123.

Brosvic, G., Dihoff, R., & Fama, J. (2002). Age-related susceptibility to the Muller-Lyer and the horizontal-vertical illusions. *Perceptual and Motor Skills, 94*, 229-234.

Basic Questions

1. How difficult did you find this task? How accurate do you think you were in this task? Looking at your individual data, do your results support the feelings you had about your performance? Explain.

2. When the line without wings and the line with wings were the same size, how often did you report the line without wings as being bigger?

3. What is the method of constant stimuli? How is it different from other psychophysical methods?

Advanced Questions

1. Describe what your data would look like if you suppose that the wings of the comparison line were drawn inward instead of outward in this demonstration.

2. In this demonstration, the method of constant stimuli was used to measure the effect of a particular type of illusion. What else could this method be used to measure?

3. Does your personal data indicate you experienced the Muller-Lyer illusion? Explain.

Discussion Question

1. Experience teaches us to expect certain perceptual relationships among stimuli. Illusions often take advantage of these expectations. Think of an everyday situation that could partly explain the Muller-Lyer illusion.

Signal Detection

Minimum time to complete this experiment: 15 minutes

Background

Much of cognitive psychology involves gathering data from experimental participants. Gathering good data is not always easy, especially when one uses a variety of people as participants. Researchers often must carefully design an experiment to be certain that participants are following the instructions and are motivated to try their best. Even despite these efforts, experimental results can be contaminated by individual differences if the researcher does not properly analyze the data.

For example, consider two participants in visual detection of a faint target. The researcher wants to explore a property of the visual system, so he/she presents a visual stimulus and asks the participants to report whether they saw the target. After 50 trials, participant A reports seeing the target 25 times and participant B reports detection 17 times. Did participant A do better? Not necessarily, perhaps participant A is simply more prone to report seeing the target and participant B is more conservative. That is, the two participants may have equivalent visual systems, but differences in reporting. Reports of simple detection do not allow the researcher to compare participants' results.

A better experiment is a modification of the one above. Have two kinds of trials, one with the target present and one with the target absent. Again have subjects report whether they saw the target. There are four statistics to be calculated from this experiment. Trials in which a participant correctly detects the target are called *hits*. The trials in which the target was there but participants did not detect it are called *misses*. If a participant reports seeing the target when it was not actually there, he/she has made a mistake (*false alarm*). A trial in which the participant correctly reports that the target was not present is a *correct rejection*.

Suppose that after 100 trials (50 for target present and 50 for target absent) the researcher again finds that on the trials in which the target was in fact present, participant A reports seeing it 25 times and participant B 17 times. Who is doing better? It depends on the frequency of false alarms. If participant A has 25 false alarms and participant B has 5 false alarms, then B is better than A at distinguishing the trials in which the target is present from the trials in which the target is absent. That is, in this case, A seems to often guess that the target is there, but he/she is wrong (false alarm) as often as right (hit). B is more selective about saying he/she detects the target, but rarely says the target is there when it is not. Thus, B is doing better.

This type of analysis suggests that you need to consider two numbers, hits and false alarms to really be able to compare performance across subjects. Fortunately, you can combine the numbers in a careful way to produce a single number that gives an indication of the *sensitivity* of the participant to the presence of the target. The calculation is structured so that, with certain assumptions, it will not matter whether a participant takes a conservative or liberal approach to claiming to detect the target. There are several measures of sensitivity, the most commonly used one being d' (d-prime), which is based on signal detection theory.

A discussion of the algorithms for calculating sensitivity is beyond the scope of this experiment [see Macmillan & Creelman, (1991) for further discussion]. Instead, you will participate in an experiment that measures sensitivity.

Instructions

A window will appear that fills nearly the entire screen, and a smaller window will appear with abbreviated instructions. Close the instructions window. You can open it again later from the *CogLab Info.* menu.

Press the *space bar* to start a trial. A group of randomly placed dots (sort of like a "star field") will appear. The number of random dots varies from trial to trial. Also, on some trials (target present) an additional set of ten dots arranged in a straight line that slants downward from left to right is randomly placed among the dot field. On the other trials (target absent), the line is not included. Your task is to report whether the target is present or absent.

If you think the target is present, press the / key. If you think the target is not present, press the *z* key. You will be given feedback on whether you were correct. In addition, on the trials in which the target was actually present, a green line will connect the target dots after you make your decision. Look for the dots along this line so you will learn what the target looks like but the target will be randomly placed on the screen from trial to trial. There are a total of 60 trials, twenty trials for each number of random dots. Half of the trials have the target present, while the target is absent on the other half of the trials.

At the end of the experiment, the experiment window will close and a new window will appear that displays your data as a table and a plot (if appropriate) and provides an explanation of the experiment and results. You can print this information, save it as an html file, or save it in CogLab format. The latter format can be re-opened with CogLab on a CD and by your instructor who may want to combine data from students in your class.

Additional References

Santhi, N., & Reeves, A. (2004). The roles of distractor noise and target certainty in search: A signal detection model. *Vision Research, 44*, 1235-1256.

Maylor, E., & Rabbitt, P. (1987). Effect of alcohol on rate of forgetting. *Psychopharmacology, 91*, 230-235.

Kerkhof, G., & Uhlenbroek, J. (1981). P3 latency in threshold signal detection. *Biological Psychology, 13*, 89-105.

Basic Questions

1. Define the following terms in relation to signal detection theory: hit, miss, false alarm, and correct rejection.

2. Imagine your individual sensitivity measures for each of the three conditions are greater than those of all of your classmates? What does this mean in terms or your ability to detect targets in comparison to your classmates?

3. If an individual's hit rate is .79 and his/her correct rejection rate is .71, what is his/her miss rate and his/her false alarm rate?

Advanced Questions

1. While going over some experimental results from a signal detection study, you notice an individual's hit rate is .98. What does this tell you about his/her sensitivity measure?

2. Signal detection theory assumes that a signal is always accompanied by a certain amount of noise. Identify at least two sources of noise for the detection of an audio signal.

3. Name at least three jobs that must accurately detect signals to effectively do the job. This means that signal detection methods could be used to evaluate performance.

Discussion Question

1. The C statistic is also known as the response criterion. This is the amount of evidence an individual requires to make a target-present response. What does a negative C statistic mean? What does a positive C statistic mean? What factors can influence someone's response criterion?

Visual Search

Minimum time to complete this experiment: 20 minutes

Background

This experiment explores aspects of attention in a visual-search task. It is a classic experiment that makes strikingly clear the time needed to bring attention to bear on different regions of visual space. The basic idea is to ask a participant to search a visual image for a particular item and to respond as quickly as possible once they find the item, or to respond as quickly as possible when they are certain the item is not in the image. This type of experiment was used to develop a popular theory of attention (Treisman & Gelade, 1980).

Searches are divided into two types, those that require selective use of attention and those that do not. In the latter, the target item seems to pop-out of the display and the participant can respond quickly. Notably, this pop-out effect allows the participant to respond quickly even when the number of other (distractor) items is increased. In the other type of display, it seems that the participant is forced to study each item individually until the target item is found. In these cases, the target item does not pop-out and search time increases with the number of distractor items. Controlling whether attention is needed or not is accomplished by the type of target and distractor items.

In the experiment below, the target is always a green circle. For the feature condition, the distractors are always blue squares. As you will see, the green circle seems to pop out of the image to quickly identify the location of the target. To require attention, the distractor items are made more complex. Some of the distractors are green squares while others are blue circles. Because some of the distractors are green, the green target circle no longer pops out and the participant must search through all the items to find the one that is both green and a circle. This type of search is called a *conjunctive search* because the target is a conjunction of features in the distractors.

Instructions

A window will appear that fills nearly the entire screen, and a smaller window will appear with abbreviated instructions. Close the instructions window. You can open it again later from the *CogLab Info.* menu.

Press the space bar to start the first trial. A fixation dot will appear in the middle of the window. Stare at it. A short time later (less than a second), circles and squares of various colors will appear on the screen. Your task is to determine if there is a *green circle* among the shapes. When you see a green circle, press the / key on your keyboard as quickly as possible. When you are certain there is not a green circle in the window, press the z key on your keyboard, again as quickly as possible.

After pressing the z or / key, press the *space* bar to start the next trial.

The feature and conjunctive trials consist of approximately 48 trials each. If you make a mistake (e.g., say "Present" when you should have said "Absent"), that trial is repeated later in the experiment, so you may actually run more than 48 trials. You can also discard a trial by pressing the *t* key instead of *z* or */*. Discarding is appropriate if, after starting a trial, you sneeze, zone out, or are otherwise distracted. Discarded trials will be repeated later.

In every trial, your goal is simply to determine if a green circle is present. If it is press */*, if it is not press *z*. If you are frequently incorrect (feedback is given when you are incorrect), try to delay your response until you are more certain that you are correct.

At the end of the experiment, the experiment window will close and a new window will appear that displays your data as a table and a plot (if appropriate) and provides an explanation of the experiment and results. You can print this information, save it as an html file, or save it in CogLab format. The latter format can be re-opened with CogLab on a CD and by your instructor who may want to combine data from students in your class.

Additional References

Herd, S., & O'Reilly, R. (2005). Serial visual search from a parallel model. *Vision Research, 45*, 2987-2992.

Bichot, N., Rossi, A. & Desimone, R. (2005). Parallel and serial neural mechanisms for visual search in macaque area V4. *Science, 308*, 529-534.

Wolfe, J. (1994). Guided search 2.0: A revised model of visual search. *Psychonomic Bulletin & Review, 1*, 202-238.

Wolfe, J., Cave, K., & Franzel, S. (1989). Guided search: An alternative to the feature integration model for visual search. *Journal of Experimental Psychology: Human Perception and Performance, 15*, 419-433.

Basic Questions

1. Did you find the feature search or the conjunctive search to be more difficult? Why?

2. A common observation within visual-search tasks, such as the one in this demonstration, is that the conjunctive absent condition takes about twice as long as the conjunctive present condition. Why would this be the case?

3. Why does increasing the number of distractors typically slow reaction-times in a conjunctive search but not in a feature search?

Advanced Questions

1. Identify two products/items in which applying the concepts of visual search would be useful.

2. Visual search is a process we use many times throughout the day. Go back through your day and identify a few of the instances in which you had to employ a visual search process.

3. For each of the instances you identified in advanced question two, identify the features of your target and categorize them as unique to the target or shared by the distractors. How many distractors were there? How long did your search take and was this search time consistent or inconsistent with the predictions of visual search?

Discussion Question

1. What role does attention play in visual search?

Brain Asymmetry

Minimum time to complete this experiment: 10 minutes

Background

You may have heard that each person has two distinct hemispheres of the brain, with different capabilities. For example, the sensory signals from the left side of your body are sent to the right hemisphere of your brain and the sensory signals from the right side of your body are sent to the left hemisphere of your brain. Likewise, control of your right arm and leg is via your left hemisphere and control of your left arm and leg is via your right hemisphere. More notable cognitive differences also exist.

The left hemisphere is said to deal with language and analytical thought, while the right hemisphere is said to deal with spatial relations and creativity. The basis for these claims about cognition comes from investigations of clinical patients who, usually to control a serious case of epilepsy, underwent surgery that separated their left and right hemispheres. (This surgery prevented epileptic seizures from passing from one hemisphere to the other.) Careful studies of these split-brain patients revealed fascinating properties about how the brain was organized. A patient asked to fix on a spot on a screen could verbally report words flashed on the right side of the screen. (Those words were sent to the left hemisphere.) The patient could not say the word if it was flashed on the left side of the screen (thus sent to the right hemisphere). Notably, the patient could identify, by picking up with the *left hand*, a physical item matching a word flashed on the left side of the screen.

Subsequent work showed a variety of differences between the brain hemispheres, and some researchers concluded that even people without split brains effectively have two competing brains. These conclusions were picked up by the popular press, and one now sees a variety of claims that schools should nurture one brain side instead of another, or that different types of therapy should be used to strengthen an undeveloped hemisphere.

Some of these claims appear in very odd places. For example, unrelated research suggests that Mozart's music stimulates creativity and intelligence in children. One CD jacket claims that Mozart's music stimulates the left brain to improve logical skills. It suggests positioning the speakers on the child's right side (presumably so the sound goes to the left brain). It is nice music and may help improve logical skills, but the left brain/right brain difference does not necessarily have anything to do with it. Moreover, sound will go in both ears and reach both hemispheres, so positioning the speakers on one side versus another cannot possibly make much difference.

As it turns out, many experiments fail to find much difference at all between the two hemispheres in normals (individuals without split-brain surgery). This is not to suggest that there are no differences, but the functional significance of these differences may be very slight. Moreover, when such differences do exist, they tend to be strongest for right-handed males. Females and left-handed individuals tend to not show brain-side effects nearly as well.

This experiment uses a technique devised by Levy, Heller, Banich, & Burton (1983) (also see Rueckert, 2005) for demonstrating differences between the hemispheres of a normal subject's brain. The stimuli involve chimeric faces. A chimeric face is made by taking two different faces, dividing them in half, and combining the left side of one face with the right side of the other face to make a combined, chimeric, face.

The subject then views two such chimeric faces and must decide which one more strongly demonstrates a particular quality (e.g., happiness, age, attractiveness). If the chimeric faces are constructed so that the two halves differ in the quality of the rated characteristic and so that the information goes to different brain hemispheres, then the choices made by subjects should show a bias toward information that goes to the right hemisphere, which seems to be more involved than the left hemisphere in making judgments about faces.

Significantly, the expected effect should be weaker for left-handed people than for right-handed people because the former show fewer differences between the left and right hemispheres.

Instructions

A small window will appear that asks you to indicate whether you are right-handed or left-handed. There are several definitions of handedness, but you might report which hand you typically use to write. After answering the handedness question, a window will appear that fills nearly the entire screen, and a smaller window will appear with abbreviated instructions. Close the instructions window. You can open it again later from the *CogLab Info.* menu.

Click on the space bar to start a trial. Two chimeric faces will appear. Choose the face that seems youngest. To indicate that the chimeric face on the top appears younger, press the *i* key. Press the *k* key to indicate that the chimeric face on the bottom appears younger. With your keypress, a green box will be drawn around the selected chimeric face. This indicates that the computer noted your choice. You can change your choice if you wish.

You will not receive feedback on whether you were correct in your choice. Indeed, there are no absolutely correct or incorrect answers, simply report what seems correct to you. After you are satisfied with your choice, press the space bar for the next trial.

At the end of the experiment, the experiment window will close and a new window will appear that displays your data as a table and a plot (if appropriate) and provides an explanation of the experiment and results. You can print this information, save it as an html file, or save it in CogLab format. The latter format can be re-opened with CogLab on a CD and by your instructor who may want to combine data from students in your class.

References

Rueckert, L. (2005). A web-based study of cerebral asymmetry for perception of emotion. *Behavior Research Methods, 37 (2)*, 271-276.

Kanwisher, N., McDermott, J., & Chun, M. (1997). The fusiform face area: A module in human extrastriate cortex specialized for face perception. *The Journal of Neuroscience, 17 (11)*, 4302-4311.

Levy. J., Heller, W., Banich, M., & Burton, L. (1983). Asymmetry of perception in free viewing of chimeric faces. *Brain & Cognition, 2*, 404-419.

Gazzaniga, M. S., Bogen, J. E., & Sperry, R. W. (1965). Observations on visual perception after disconnection of the cerebral hemispheres in man. *Brain, 88*, Part 2, 221-236.

Basic Questions

1. Does your data provide evidence that you have an asymmetric brain? Explain your answer.

2. Describe another experiment that would test for brain asymmetry. It should be different from this experiment and the split-brain language experiment already described.

3. What skills/processes are primarily associated with the left hemisphere? What about the right hemisphere?

Advanced Questions

1. What types of professions might benefit from using what we know about brain asymmetry?

2. Describe a task that might be more difficult for a split-brain patient than a normal individual.

3. The interpretation of the experimental results relies on a comparison between the data from right-handed participants as well as left-handed participants. Why is this the case?

Discussion Question

1. Why might it be advantageous for us to have a brain in which some processes are specific to one hemisphere?

Blind Spot

Minimum time to complete this experiment: 35 minutes

Background

Your eyes contain a dense set of receptors that are sensitive to light energy. These receptors convert light energy into electrical energy, which eventually is transferred to your nervous system and your brain. These receptors, however, are not distributed evenly across your eye. There is a central location, called the fovea, where the receptors are very densely packed. Generally, when you stare at an object you are arranging your eyes so that the object's image falls on the foveae of your eyes. There are fewer receptors outside the fovea. In fact, in some places there are no receptors at all.

There is a place in each eye where the optic nerve exits the back of the eye to send information to the brain. This "hole" is called the optic disk. It contains no light sensitive receptors. As a result, any light that falls on this part of the eye is undetected and invisible to you. Functionally, this location on the eye is called the blind spot.

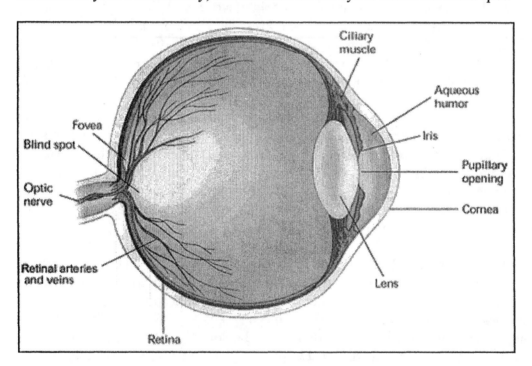

You have probably never noticed your blind spots (one in each eye). There are several reasons for this. First, each blind spot is far away from its eye's fovea. Because the fovea is typically where you are "looking," you would not generally notice that something has disappeared into a blind spot. Second, when you view the world with two eyes, one eye can compensate for the other eye's blind spot. Light that falls into the blind spot of one eye generally does not fall on the blind spot of the other eye. Third, your brain only processes the presence of information, not the absence. Your brain does not notice a "hole" in the information it receives from the eye. It simply works with the information it receives. In a similar way, the brain does not observe that we are unable to view ultraviolet light. It has no knowledge about missing information.

With the proper experiment, however, it is possible to identify and map the blind spot, which is the purpose of this experiment. You will probably be surprised at how large the blind spot is. It covers a large part of your visual field. The experiment used here is similar to a test used by eye doctors to identify visual scotomas (damaged spots in the retina of your eye). Should you consistently find "holes" in your data other than the blind spot, you may want to see an eye doctor.

Instructions

A window will fill the entire screen, and a smaller window will appear with abbreviated instructions. Close the instructions window. You can open it again later from the *CogLab Info.* menu.

A small blue fixation square will appear on the far left of the screen. The experiment is designed to map the blind spot of your right eye. Close your left eye or cover it with your hand or a patch. Fix on the small square with your right eye. Try to sit so that your head is centered directly in front of the fixation square. Press the *space* bar key to start a trial. A white dot will appear somewhere on the screen. Simultaneously, the fixation point will turn green. Your task is to report whether you see the white dot or not, all while keeping your right eye fixed on the fixation square.

If you see the dot, press the *m* key. If you do not see the dot, press the *n* key. Either of the keys you press will produce written feedback at the location of the fixation point. This is simply to indicate that the computer received your response. If the response is not what you intended (e.g., you pressed *m* when you meant to press *n*), just press the intended key. The computer will keep your last response as the response for that trial. Do not move your eye from the fixation square when you make this judgment. Press the *space* bar key to start the next trial when you are ready.

There are a total of 300 trials. That may sound like a lot, but each trial takes only a couple of seconds. You can take a break if you wish, but try to stay seated in the same position when you resume the experiment. If you move around, your blind spot will move with you and the data will be a mix of the two positions you take. Also, be careful to make accurate judgments of whether you see or do not see the dot. If you try to go too fast, the computer will warn you to slow down. Most importantly, keep your right eye fixed on the small fixation square. If you move your eye around, be sure to go back to the fixation square before making your judgment about seeing or not seeing a dot.

The data are given in two different formats. First, the experimental window will show a full array of dots colored green and red. These dots are in the locations you just viewed during the experiment. Any dot colored green is one that you reported as visible. Any dot colored red is one that you reported as not visible. You should find that there is a patch of red dots near the middle of the array. These are dots whose image fell on the blind spot of your eye. Its precise location varies a bit among observers and varies a lot depending on how far you are seated from the monitor.

The second display is in a new window that appears and displays your data as a table and provides an explanation of the experiment and results. You can print this information, save it as an html file, or save it in CogLab format. The latter format can be re-opened with CogLab on a CD and by your instructor who may want to combine data from students in your class.

Additional References

Matsumoto, M., & Komatsu, H. (2005). Neural responses in the macaque V1 to bar stimuli with various lengths presented on the blind spot. *Journal of Neurophysiology, 93,* 2374-2387.

Kawabata, N. (1982). Visual information processing at the blind spot. *Perceptual and Motor Skills, 55,* 95-104.

Cumming, G., & Friend, H. (1980). Perception at the blind spot and tilt aftereffect. *Perception, 9,* 233-238.

Basic Questions

1. Describe the location of your blind spot identified by this demonstration. Was its location consistent with what was expected?

2. What is the cause of your blind spot?

3. In this demonstration, what would affect the size of an individual's blind spot?

Advanced Questions

1. Why is it important to keep your left eye closed for this demonstration to work?

2. Could you change anything about the target stimulus to overcome your blind spot? Explain.

3. Describe a situation in which an individual might be susceptible to missing something in the environment because of their blind spot.

Discussion Question

1. Your blind spot typically goes unnoticed. Describe a few of the reasons why this is the case.

Receptive Fields

Minimum time to complete this experiment: 25 minutes (often more)

Background

A fundamental tenet of cognitive science is that the mind can be understood by studying the brain. The brain consists of billions of individual cells (neurons), whose combined behavior corresponds to what we call cognition. Because of the immense number of neurons and their complicated connections, it is difficult to relate the behavior of an individual neuron with human behavior (e.g., seeing a red apple).

A concept that helps make that connection, in certain cases, is the *receptive field*. Basically, the receptive field of a neuron consists of any stimulus that *changes* the neuron's firing rate. By definition, every neuron has a receptive field, although the receptive fields for some neurons are very complicated. The concept of a receptive field is most useful in those parts of the brain that are tied to specific senses (e.g., touch, audition, vision, taste) or to motor control. For neurons sensitive to visual information, for example, the receptive field describes how spatial patterns of light influence the neuron's behavior. It is often the case that a neuron responds only when light falls within a certain part of the visual field. Moreover, the light can have excitatory or inhibitory effects, depending on where it falls in the receptive field. Identifying the region of the receptive field and the excitatory and inhibitory parts provides a good deal of information about the role of the neuron in visual perception.

In a neurophysiological study of visual receptive fields (and there are many), a researcher typically inserts an electrode into a neuron to record its electrical potential (including action potentials). The researcher then presents visual stimuli to the animal and records the cellular responses. By noting changes in the electrical potential (or in the number of action potentials), the researcher can determine if light at a particular location is: (a) excitatory, (b) inhibitory, or (c) outside the receptive field and thus neither excitatory nor inhibitory. By carefully watching the cell's behavior as the stimulus changes, the researcher can map out the receptive field of a neuron.

Knowledge about neural receptive fields is of great significance for understanding perception. For example, neurons close to the retinas of your eyes have (relatively) circularly shaped receptive fields. For some neurons, the center of this circle is excitatory, while the surround is inhibitory. Other neurons switch the locations of excitation and inhibition. Some neurons in area V1 of the cortex are sensitive to light-to-dark edges of a specific orientation. Other neurons in area V1 are sensitive to light-to-dark edges but are also sensitive to dark-to-light edges of the same orientation. The properties of these neurons play a fundamental role in theories of visual perception.

This experiment provides you with the opportunity to map out receptive fields. Your task is to find a stimulus that drives an unknown receptive field. Do not take the properties of the virtual neurons too literally. The receptive fields are caricatures of true receptive fields; they do not take into account much of the underlying neurophysiology. This caveat aside, the experiment will hopefully introduce you to the concept of receptive fields.

Instructions

A window will appear that includes a plot, a large black area, and buttons. A smaller window will also appear with abbreviated instructions. Close the instructions window. You can open it again later from the *CogLab Info.* menu.

On the main window, the large black area is a canvas for drawing the stimulus. Here you place stimuli that are to be presented to the virtual visual system. On the top left is a plot that shows the response of the cell to the drawn stimulus. The plot is updated every half a second. Position the stimulus by dragging the mouse (click and move the mouse) in the black drawing canvas. Change the stimulus shape by selecting from the pull-down choices. Adjust the stimulus size with the sliders.

Your task is to create and position a stimulus that generates a response from the neuron that is at least 50% of its maximal response. Once you have that stimulus, you can move on to the next trial. This is more difficult than it sounds. You must first identify where the receptive field is located on the canvas. It may be best to use a small filled dot to do this. The text in the upper right part of the window identifies the type of receptive field present (see the images below), and it gives information about how strongly the current drawn pattern drives the cell.

The first four trials are for practice. The practice trials are just like the test trials, except you can always reveal the true shape of the receptive field by clicking on the *Show RF* button. Use the practice trials to see the receptive field and explore how light patterns correspond to electrical potentials. A shown receptive field is represented on the drawing canvas by a green (excitatory) region and a red (inhibitory) region. The locations of the green and red pixels correspond to the location in visual space of the receptive field. With the mouse, place a filled circle in the middle of the green region. You should see that the plot of electrical potential rises and the number of spikes increases. The spikes plotted intermittently correspond to action potentials. Action potential frequency increases as electrical potential increases, but action potentials can also occur without a stimulus.

Try changing the size of the circle so that it fills most of the green area. You should find that the neuron gives a strong response. When the response gets above 50% of the cell's maximum response, the *Next Trial* button becomes activated. Before starting the next trial, increase the size of the filled circle to cover some of the red region as well. You will find that the electrical potential is smaller and there are fewer action potentials. When the stimulus covers all of the red and the green, you should find that the neuron does not respond to the stimulus any differently than it responds to a blank screen.

The receptive field types and their shapes are shown in the figure below. The simple and complex receptive fields have similar shapes, but the complex receptive field is actually, well, more complex than can be drawn. A complex receptive field can respond to light on either side of its receptive field, but it does not respond well to light on *both* sides of its receptive field. A simple receptive field is sensitive to light on only one, fixed side.

On-center,
off-surround

Off-center,
on-surround

Simple or
complex

The receptive field will be randomly located on the canvas drawing surface. Your task is to find its location and choose a stimulus shape and size that will get the neuron to respond strongly. Only then can you move on to the next trial. Each receptive field is presented once, in random order.

At the end of the experiment, the experiment window will close and a new window will appear that displays your data as a table and a plot (if appropriate) and provides an explanation of the experiment and results. You can print this information, save it as an html file, or save it in CogLab format. The latter format can be re-opened with CogLab on a CD and by your instructor who may want to combine data from students in your class.

Additional References

Schefrin, B., Hauser, M., & Werner, J. (2004). Evidence against age-related enlargements of ganglion cell receptive field centers under scotopic conditions. *Vision Research, 44,* 423-428.

Georgeson, M., & Scott-Samuel, N. (2000). Spatial resolution and receptive field height of motion sensors in human vision. *Vision Research, 40,* 745-758.

Wiesel, T., & Hubel, D. (1963). Single-cell responses in striate cortex of kittens deprived of vision in one eye. *Journal of Neurophysiology, 26,* 1002-1017.

Basic Questions

1. In this demonstration, which cell's receptive field was the most difficult to map? Does your data support your assessment? Why?

2. What physiological measure is used to identify a neuron's activation?

3. What shape of light induced high levels of activation for each of the following types of cells: on-center, off-surround cells, off-center, on-surround cells, simple cells, and complex cells?

Advanced Questions

1. What feature of an object or a picture would simple cells be useful in identifying?

2. When trying to find various constellations in the night sky, which type of receptive field would be most responsive?

3. Consider a white square on a black background. Where would you place an on-center, off-surround cell if trying to maximize its response activation?

Discussion Question

1. This demonstration showed that certain neurons in the visual system are sensitive to specific patterns of light. What stimulus properties might trigger responses in neurons related to other modalities (i.e., audition, smell, taste, and touch)?

Metacontrast Masking

Minimum time to complete this experiment: 35 minutes

Background

Masking refers to a class of phenomena in which presentation of one stimulus (the mask) can impair performance on some task that requires judgment about another stimulus (the target). Visual masking plays two roles in cognitive science. First, masking is used to investigate properties of the visual system. By identifying the way in which the target and mask stimuli influence each other, vision scientists are able to deduce details about the underlying mechanisms involved in visual perception. Second, visual masking is used to indirectly restrict systems involved in information processing of visual stimuli.

The logic of this type of approach is that the mask can halt further processing of the target and one can thereby explore the order and time course of many information-processing systems. A special subset of this approach is based on evidence that people with various types of cognitive disorders may respond differently than normal people under some masking conditions. Thus, masking has been proposed as a simple method for detecting some disorders and as a means of specifying the underlying mechanisms for those disorders.

Both the target and mask stimuli are usually very brief (often less than 200 milliseconds). Despite its short duration, if the target stimulus is presented by itself, it is clearly visible and it is easy for observers to perform whatever judgment is required of them. What is interesting is that the subsequent presentation of a mask stimulus, even a hundred milliseconds after the target has turned off, can make the observer's task of judging something about the target exceedingly difficult. When this effect was first noted by Stigler (1910), it forced the field of perceptual psychology to realize that the processing of visual information took time and could be interrupted. Backward masking has been used to identify details of the perceptual and cognitive processes involved in building percepts and judgments.

Metacontrast masking is a specific type of masking in which the target and mask have no overlapping contours and the mask follows the target in time. A surprising finding in studies of metacontrast masking is that when performance on some judgment about the target is plotted against the stimulus onset asynchrony (SOA) between the target and mask, the resulting curve is U-shaped. Performance is generally quite good when the mask immediately follows the target. Performance is also generally good for very long (greater than 200 milliseconds) SOAs. For SOAs between 60 and 100 milliseconds, however, performance is often quite poor. Some observers even report that they do not see the target at all.

The effect of the mask on the target sometimes gets stronger as the target and mask are separated in time, which is contrary to many simple models of visual perception.

Investigations of the U-shaped metacontrast masking function are numerous and have identified a variety of characteristics about the visual system.

Instructions

A window will appear that fills nearly the entire screen, and a smaller window will appear with abbreviated instructions. Close the instructions window. You can open it again later from the *CogLab Info.* menu.

Click on the space bar to start a trial. A small fixation square will appear in the middle of the screen. Fix on this square. Half a second later, four rectangles will appear at the corners of an imaginary square around the fixation point. Three of the rectangles will be squares, while one will be a bit thinner than a square. The rectangles will be shown for only 30 milliseconds. In addition, a box will be drawn around each of the rectangles. The boxes will also be shown for 30 milliseconds. The timing between the rectangles and boxes varies from trial to trial. It is characterized by the stimulus onset asynchrony (SOA). This is the time between the onset of the target (rectangles) and the mask (boxes). When SOA equals zero, the rectangles and boxes will appear together. On other trials, the boxes will obviously follow the rectangles.

Your task is always the same: Report the location of the thin rectangle. Make your selection by a key-press to indicate the location. Press the *u* key to indicate the top-left position. Press the *i* key to indicate the top-right location. Press the *k* key to indicate the bottom-right location. Press the *j* key to indicate the bottom-left position. With each key-press, a rectangle will appear that corresponds to the selection you are making. You can change your choice by pressing another key. When you are satisfied with your choice, press the space bar key to start the next trial. Before the next trial begins, you will be given feedback on whether your choice was correct. You will notice an error when the rectangle corresponding to your choice changes to the actual location.

There are seven SOAs, and 30 trials for each SOA. This makes a total of 210 trials. That may sound like a lot, but each trial only takes a few seconds, so the entire experiment will not take very long. Moreover, you can take a break between trials if needed. There may be some trials in which the rectangles do not seem to appear at all. Likewise, there may be trials in which you have absolutely no idea where the thin rectangle is located. On such trials, guess the location. Do not be concerned if you often have to guess.

At the end of the experiment, the experiment window will close and a new window will appear that displays your data as a table and a plot (if appropriate) and provides an explanation of the experiment and results. You can print this information, save it as an html file, or save it in CogLab format. The latter format can be re-opened with CogLab on a CD and by your instructor who may want to combine data from students in your class.

Additional References

Francis, G., Rothmayer, M., & Hermens, F. (2004). Analysis and test of laws for backward (metacontrast) masking. *Spatial Vision, 17*, 163-185.

Kondo, H., & Komatsu, H. (2000). Suppression on neuronal responses by a metacontrast masking stimulus in monkey V4. *Neuroscience Research, 36*, 27-33.

Francis, G. (2000). Quantitative theories of metacontrast masking. *Psychological Review, 107*, 768-785.

Lachter, J., & Durgin, F. (1999). Metacontrast masking functions: A question of speed? *Journal of Experimental Psychology: Human Perception and Performance, 25*, 936-947.

Basic Questions

1. What is SOA?

2. Using your data, at what SOA was your performance the best? At what SOA was your performance the worst? Are your results consistent with the typical findings of a metacontrast masking experiment? Explain.

3. What do the findings of masking experiments tell us about visual perception?

Advanced Questions

1. Using your data, at what SOA would your performance be near perfect?

2. In this demonstration, if you identified the thin rectangle correctly 25% of the time is your performance above random guessing, below random guessing, or equal to random guessing? Explain.

3. This demonstration used a specific type of visual masking, but masking can also be utilized in other modalities. Describe a situation in which auditory masking is used or would be useful.

Discussion Question

1. Why is performance high at long and short SOAs and low at medium SOAs in metacontrast masking?

Modality Effect

Minimum time to complete this experiment: 20 minutes

Background

People often have to recall a series of items in order, such as a phone number. When the list of items is heard (as opposed to read silently), people usually are very good at remembering the final list item. This advantage in recalling just the last one or two items when the list is heard is called the modality effect.

Modality effects can be seen with presentation modalities other than auditory (hearing). Lists that are lip-read or silently mouthed also produce an advantage for the last one or two items compared to silent visual presentation.

These effects have an enormous influence on the development of sensory memory. This memory system is supposed to store raw, unanalyzed sensory input. It can be thought of as a back-up system: If the information in this store is useful, recall can be enhanced.

The best explanation is that auditory presentation leads to an additional type of information compared to visual (Neath & Surprenant, 2003). When trying to recall the last item in the list, you are more likely to be successful if you also have some information about how the list sounds.

Instructions

This experiment requires a computer that can play sounds. We recommend using headphones so that you do not disturb other people. Please make sure the volume is not too loud before you put the headphones on.

An experiment window will appear, and a smaller window will appear with abbreviated instructions. Close the instructions window. You can open it again later from the *CogLab Info.* menu.

Click on the "Next trial" button to start a trial.

On each trial, you will either see or hear the digits 1 through 9 in random order. Then, you will see the response buttons become active. Your task is to click on the buttons *in the same order* that the numbers were presented. After you have finished clicking on all the buttons to recreate the list, click on "Next trial" to start the next sequence.

Being correct means that you click on the buttons in the same order the items appeared in the sequence. There is no way to correct mistakes in button presses, so be careful in your selections. There are 30 trials.

At the end of the experiment, the experiment window will close and a new window will appear that displays your data as a table and a plot (if appropriate) and provides an explanation of the experiment and results. You can print this information, save it as an html file, or save it in CogLab format. The latter format can be re-opened with CogLab on a CD and by your instructor who may want to combine data from students in your class.

Additional References

Beaman, C. P. (2002). Inverting the modality effect in serial recall. *Quarterly Journal of Experimental Psychology A: Human Experimental Psychology, 55*, 371-389.

Crowder, R. (1986). Auditory and temporal factors in the modality effect. *Journal of Experimental Psychology: Learning, Memory, and Cognition, 12*, 268-278.

Engle, R., & Roberts, J. (1982). How long does the modality effect persist? *Bulletin of the Psychonomic Society, 19*, 343-346.

Basic Questions

1. Describe your personal data. For which list position was your recall performance the highest? For which was it the lowest?

2. Does your data show the modality effect? Why or why not?

3. What is sensory memory?

Advanced Questions

1. Using what you have learned from this demonstration, what study tips would you give to a friend who has an important exam coming up?

2. When looking up a phone number in the yellow pages, what can you do to improve your recall of that phone number later?

3. What occupations might be able to use the findings from experiments on the modality effect in their work? Explain.

Discussion Question

1. Why does the modality effect only show up for the last one or two items in the list?

Partial Report

Minimum time to complete this experiment: 20 minutes

Background

In the early beginnings of the study of psychology, researchers were interested in something called the "perceptual span." Their quest was to determine how much information could be gathered in a single percept. For example, when you read text, how many letters can you interpret in a single glance? Or, how many coins can you distinguish if you briefly glance at them? The goal was to identify the limits of perceptual abilities. A variety of ingenious studies seemed to draw similar conclusions: People could accurately report about 4.5 items from a brief percept. This fact was built into many theories of cognition until a set of experiments by George Sperling (1960) proved it wrong.

Sperling suggested that the 4.5 item limit was imposed not by the capabilities of the perceptual system, but by observers' abilities to recall items that had been seen. To test this possibility, he designed a partial-report experiment. This laboratory allows you to participate in a version of this experiment.

In Sperling's original experiment, the observer saw a three by three matrix of random letters on each trial. The letters were flashed for a very short period of time (50 milliseconds). After the letter matrix turned off, one of three tones sounded, and the observer reported the letters from the row associated with the tone. If the tone was presented directly after offset of the letters, Sperling found that observers were nearly 100% accurate in reporting letters from the indicated row.

This result destroys theories that hypothesized that percepts hold only 4 or 5 items. Because the tone was sounded after the letters disappeared, observers must be focusing on the appropriate row as it is stored in some type of *sensory store* of perceptual information. Moreover, since perfect performance is found regardless of which row is indicated, the sensory store must contain a nearly perfect representation of the total visual percept. Thus, perceptual span was not 4.5 items, but essentially every item in the visual field.

What determined perceptual span in the earlier experiments was not the limits of the perceptual system, but the time needed to report the seen items. The duration of information in the sensory store is very brief (a few hundred milliseconds) so, as observers report what they see, items in the sensory store fade away. By the time observers report on 4 or 5 items, the sensory store information is gone and recall is finished.

Sperling also found a way to measure the duration of information in the sensory store. When he increased the time between the offset of the letter matrix and the onset of the tone cue, he found that recall of letters became worse. If the tone was delayed by a full second, recall was comparable to the 4.5 items found in other experiments.

When these experimental results were reported in 1960, they revolutionized both our understanding of perception and memory and the experimental methods with which cognitive psychology was studied. There have subsequently been thousands of studies on the sensory (also called *iconic*) store and it is a part of many theories of cognition.

Instructions

This experiment requires a computer that can play sounds. We recommend using headphones so that you do not disturb other people. Please make sure the volume is not too loud before you put the headphones on.

A window will appear that fills nearly the entire screen, and a smaller window will appear with abbreviated instructions. Close the instructions window. You can open it again later from the *CogLab Info.* menu.

Press the *space* bar to start a trial. The first thing you will hear are the three tones so that you can tell which is the low pitched tone, which is the medium, and which is the high. After you have heard the tones, press the *space* bar to begin the experiment.

After you press the *space* bar, a small fixation point (an asterisk, *) will appear in the middle of the screen. Fix on this. It will disappear after one and a half seconds. Half a second later a three by three matrix of letters will be flashed for 150 milliseconds. Some time after the offset of the letter matrix, a tone will be played that indicates:

A *high* pitched tone means report the top row.
A *medium* pitched tone means report the middle row.
A *low* pitched tone means report the bottom row.

Type the letters from the indicated row. Guess if you do not know what the letters were. You can make up to three guesses for every trial.

When you are ready, press the *space* bar for the next trial. There is a total of 60 trials, with the same basic task in every one. Simply report the letters that flashed from the indicated row. As you go through the experiment, keep your eyes steady on the fixation mark, then do not move them until after the matrix disappears. There is no method for discarding a trial in this experiment, so try to make certain you are ready as you start a trial.

At the end of the experiment, the experiment window will close and a new window will appear that displays your data as a table and a plot (if appropriate) and provides an explanation of the experiment and results. You can print this information, save it as an html file, or save it in CogLab format. The latter format can be re-opened with CogLab on a CD and by your instructor who may want to combine data from students in your class.

Additional References

Fenske, M., & Stolz, J. (2001). Disengaging attention: On the locus of the cue-duration effect in partial report. *Journal of Experimental Psychology: Human Perception and Performance, 27*, 1335-1346.

Gugerty, L. (1998). Evidence from a partial report task for forgetting in dynamic spatial memory. *Human Factors, 40*, 498-508.

Di Lollo, V., & Dixon, P. (1992). Inverse duration effects in partial report. *Journal of Experimental Psychology: Human Perception and Performance, 18*, 1089-1100.

Basic Questions

1. In this experiment, how would one measure the interstimulus interval (ISI)?

2. At what ISI did you show the most accurate recall? At what ISI did you show the least accurate recall?

3. In general, participant's recall accuracy decreases as ISI increases. Explain why this relationship exists.

Advanced Questions

1. In a partial report experiment like the one in this demonstration, you are shown a 4 x 4 matrix of letters and are cued to report the letters from the first row. Assuming you recalled three of the four letters in the cued row, how many of the letters in the matrix were available in your sensory memory at the offset of the letter matrix?

2. Using your personal data, what would you predict your recall accuracy would be with a 700ms ISI?

3. You only briefly see a holiday shopping list for your family members before it gets taken away by a gust of wind. What strategy should you employ to maximize your accuracy in remembering what was on the list?

Discussion Question

1. Say you're watching television with a group of friends and something happens that makes everyone laugh but you. Afterward, everyone is talking about what made them laugh, but you do not remember seeing it at all. Is it that you did not see it or that you do not remember it? Explain.

Suffix Effect

Minimum time to complete this experiment: 20 minutes

Background

People often have to recall a series of items in order, such as a phone number. When the list of items is heard (as opposed to read silently), people usually are very good at remembering the final list item. However, if the list is followed by an irrelevant item (the suffix), recall of the final item is substantially impaired.

The suffix has to be perceived as speech in order for it to have a large effect. If the suffix is a pure tone, there is no impairment. Although the suffix has to be speech, it does not have to be a word. In general, the suffix will have a larger effect the more acoustically similar it is to the list items. One reason that the suffix effect has attracted a lot of attention is that recall is impaired even when the suffix is expected and even when the suffix is the same item (usually the digit 0) on every trial.

The best explanation is that when the suffix is perceptually grouped with the list items, it functionally increases the list length. So, rather than trying to recall a 9-item list, you are in effect recalling a 10-item list (Neath & Surprenant, 2003).

Instructions

This experiment requires a computer that can play sounds. We recommend using headphones so that you do not disturb other people. Please make sure the volume is not too loud before you put the headphones on.

A window will appear, and a second smaller window will appear with abbreviated instructions. Close the instructions window. You can open it again later from the *CogLab Info.* menu.

Click on the "Next trial" button to start a trial.

On each trial, you will hear the digits 1 through 9 in random order, followed by either a tone or the digit zero. Then you will see the response buttons become active. Your task is to click on the buttons *in the same order* that the digits were presented. After you have finished clicking on all the buttons to recreate the list, click on "Next trial" to start the next sequence.

Being correct means that you click on the buttons in the same order the items appeared in the sequence. There is no way to correct mistakes in button presses, so be careful in your selections. There are 30 trials.

At the end of the experiment, the experiment window will close and a new window will appear that displays your data as a table and a plot (if appropriate) and provides an explanation of the experiment and results. You can print this information, save it as an html file, or save it in CogLab format. The latter format can be re-opened with CogLab on a CD and by your instructor who may want to combine data from students in your class.

Additional References

Parmentier, F., Tremblay, S., & Jones, D. (2004). Exploring the suffix effect in serial visuospatial short-term memory. *Bulletin & Review, 11,* 289-295.

Penney, C. (1985). Elimination of the suffix effect on preterminal list items with unpredictable list length: Evidence for a dual model of suffix effects. *Journal of Experimental Psychology: Learning, Memory, and Cognition, 11,* 229-247.

Watkins, M., & Watkins, O. (1974). A tactile suffix effect. *Memory & Cognition, 2,* 176-180.

Basic Questions

1. What is the current explanation of the suffix effect that was given in the text?

2. Did your recall performance vary based on whether the target list was followed by the tone or the digit? Did you show the suffix effect? Explain.

3. What property of the suffix determines the magnitude of its effect in recall performance?

Advanced Questions

1. One of your parents has just listed some items for your brother to get at the grocery store. What could you do to make his recall of these items difficult?

2. Using your personal data, calculate your suffix effect.

3. You have forgotten your password (a sequence of numbers and letters) for your home security system, so you call your security provider to get it. They read you the password over the phone and then ask you if there is anything else they can do for you. You say no, thank them, and hang up. Assuming you try to remember the password instead of writing it down, what was problematic about this phone call regarding your future recall performance for your password?

Discussion Question

1. If you are orally given information that you want to remember later, discuss some things you can do to maximize your recall performance.

Brown-Peterson

Minimum time to complete this experiment: 20 minutes

Background

In the 1940s, memory loss was widely considered to be the result of new information interfering with previously learned information. In the late 1950s, two groups of researchers (one named Brown and a husband and wife team named Peterson) published data that forced a new interpretation of human memory.

Parenthetically, it is interesting to note the instructions that Peterson & Peterson (1959, p. 194) gave to their subjects: *"Please sit against the back of your chair so that you are comfortable. You will not be shocked during this experiment."* One can infer that it was common to give electric shocks to human subjects back in the 1950s.

In the memory task, the participant viewed a trigram of consonants (e.g., GKT, WCH,...) and then performed a number of algebraic computations (e.g., counting backward by 3s) for less than 20 seconds. The data showed that recall of the trigram was less likely as the participant worked on the algebraic computations for longer durations.

Solving math problems seems to be very different from recalling consonant trigrams, so it was unlikely that there was any interference to disturb the memory of the trigram. The conclusion was that there exists a short-term memory (STM) system that holds information for several seconds. Without an active effort by the participant, information in STM fades away (but see Keppel & Underwood, 1962, for an alternate explanation). Performing the distractor task prevented the participant from actively rehearsing the trigram. STM is now a fundamental part of most theories of cognitive psychology.

Instructions

A window will appear that fills nearly the entire screen, and a smaller window will appear with abbreviated instructions. Close the instructions window. You can open it again later from the *CogLab Info.* menu.

Click on the space bar to start a trial. Position your hands on the keyboard so that one finger can hit the *f* key and another can hit the *j* key. In the middle of the screen, a trigram of letters will appear for two seconds. You will then be given a sequence of letter strings and must classify each item as a word (press the *j* key) or a nonword (press the *f* key). The duration of time spent classifying the letter strings will vary from one to twenty-one seconds. You need to respond quickly enough to keep up with the sequence.

After correct completion of the classification task, you will be prompted to recall the consonant trigram. Using the keyboard, type in the letters, in the correct order, that appeared before the classification task. After you have entered your guess, and are ready for the next trial, press the space bar again.

For the trial to count, you must have correctly classified almost all the letter strings as words or nonwords. If you make any mistakes, the trial will be repeated later in the experiment. The rate of the sequence will change from trial to trial. It will become slower if you make a mistake and faster if you get it correct. To finish the experiment you must apply yourself to the word-nonword classification task. There are a total of 18 trials that must be run to finish the experiment.

At the end of the experiment, the experiment window will close and a new window will appear that displays your data as a table and a plot (if appropriate) and provides an explanation of the experiment and results. You can print this information, save it as an html file, or save it in CogLab format. The latter format can be re-opened with CogLab on a CD and by your instructor who may want to combine data from students in your class.

Additional References

Sebastian, M., Menor, J,& Elosua, R. (2001). Patterns of errors in short-term forgetting in AD and aging. *Memory, 9*, 223-231.

Nairne, J., Whiteman, H., & Kelley, M. (1999). Short-term forgetting of order under conditions of reduced interference. *Quarterly Journal of Experimental Psychology A: Human Experimental Psychology, 52*, 241-251.

Puckett, J., & Lawson, W. (1989). Absence of adult age differences in forgetting in the Brown-Peterson task. *Acta Psychologica, 72*, 159-175.

Basic Questions

1. In the Peterson and Peterson (1959) study, what was equivalent to the word non-word distractor task used in this demonstration?

2. At what distractor duration was your performance best? What duration was your performance the worst?

3. What is the function of the distractor task in the Brown-Peterson paradigm?

4. To what was the Brown-Peterson data attributed?

Advanced Questions

1. Using your personal data, at would distractor duration would you predict your recall performance to be approximately 15%?

2. Utilizing your understanding of the Brown-Peterson data, what type of environment would you suggest for someone trying to learn new material?

3. Do you or anyone you know like to study with the television or the radio on? Now that you have done this experiment, what do you think about this practice? Explain

Discussion Question

1. Other than the explanation given in Basic Question # 4, what else could have explained the data?

Position Error

Minimum time to complete this experiment: 20 minutes

Background

Many tasks require people to remember not only a set of items but also the order of the items. For example, a telephone number is meaningful only if the items are recalled in the correct order. When people do not recall an item in its correct order, the errors they make are systematic.

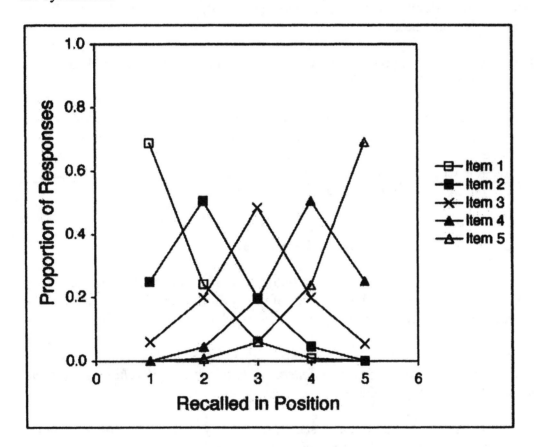

The graph above shows what these systematic errors would look like when people try to recall a five-item list in order. Most of the time, the items are recalled in the correct position. So, the line marked "Item 1" has its largest value at position 1; the line marked "Item 2" has its largest value at position 2; and so on. When an order error is made, the graph shows that the item is most likely to be recalled either 1 position too soon or 1 position too late. So, when Item 3 is not recalled in position 3, it is most likely to be recalled in position 2 or position 4. Results like these have important implications for theories of memory. If all you look at is percent correct, then you might think that forgetting means that the information is lost from the memory system. However, you are still remembering something about the item: You usually recall the item in a position adjacent to the correct position.

Instructions

An experiment window will appear, and a smaller window will appear with abbreviated instructions. Close the instructions window. You can open it again later from the *CogLab Info.* menu.

Start a trial by clicking on the Next trial button. On the left of the window, a sequence of 7 letters will appear, with each letter presented for one second. After the full sequence has been presented, the buttons on the right will show labels for items just shown. Your task is to click on the buttons in the same order that the letters were presented. If you think the first letter was M, click on the button labeled M first. If you think the sixth letter was F, click on the button labeled F sixth.

After you have finished clicking on all the buttons to recreate the list, click on Next trial to start the next sequence. There are 20 trials.

At the end of the experiment, the experiment window will close and a new window will appear that displays your data as a table and a plot (if appropriate) and provides an explanation of the experiment and results. You can print this information, save it as an html file, or save it in CogLab format. The latter format can be re-opened with CogLab on a CD and by your instructor who may want to combine data from students in your class.

Additional References

Smyth, M., Hay, D., Hitch, G., & Horton, N. (2005). Serial position memory in the visual-spatial domain: Reconstructing sequences of unfamiliar faces. *Quarterly Journal of Experimental Psychology A: Human Experimental Psychology, 58*, 909-930.

Davis, C. & Bowers, J. (2004). What do letter migration errors reveal about letter position coding in visual word recognition? *Journal of Experimental Psychology: Human Perception and Performance, 30*, 923-941.

Maylor, E. (2002). Serial position effects in semantic memory: Reconstructing the order of verses of hymns. *Psychonomic Bulletin & Review, 9*, 816-820.

Basic Questions

1. When trying to recall a list of items in order, what are the two most common position errors?

2. What does a position error analysis tell about memory as compared to an overall performance analysis?

3. What target position did you most accurately recall? What target position did you have the most trouble with at recall?

Advanced Questions

1. Look at your data. What items in the list seem to have related response patterns?

2. If you plotted item number on the x-axis and percent correct on the y-axis, what would the graph look like (assuming the errors follow the predicted pattern)?

3. Imagine you're completing a history assignment and one of the questions asks you to complete a timeline for the prominent historical events discussed in class. You know you have all the important events down, but your instructor tells you you've made one error. The good news is your instructor allows you to correct your error if you can find it. Where is the best place to look for your error? What type of errors should you keep an eye out for?

Discussion Question

1. Many people report that it is easier to recall the number sequences for the early trials of the experiment as compared to the trials that occur toward the end of the experiment. Why do you think this might be the case?

Sternberg Search

Minimum time to complete this experiment: 20 minutes

Background

Many researchers of memory believe that there exists a short-term memory (STM) system that holds information for a few seconds. If the information in STM is not transferred to long term memory (LTM) for more permanent storage, it vanishes. As evidence of the existence of STM grew, researchers started to explore its properties. In a series of articles starting in 1966, Saul Sternberg developed an experimental approach to explore how information was retrieved from STM.

The basic approach is simple. Subjects were shown a short (one to six items) list of numbers and asked to memorize them. After putting them to memory, a probe number was shown. The probe number was either one of the numbers in the list or a new number. The subject was to respond as quickly as possible, indicating whether the probe number was in the list or not. The reaction time of the subject should reflect the time spent searching STM to determine whether the probe number is part of the list. By varying the number of items in the list, Sternberg hypothesized that he could test several theories of STM search.

For example, some neural network theories of memory suggest that every item in memory can be accessed simultaneously due to the parallel nature of search in these networks. If such a search took place in STM, one would expect the reaction times *not* to vary as the number of items (memory set size) increased.

On the other hand, if memory search required consideration of each item in succession, the reaction times should increase with memory set size because the subject will, on average, have to search through more items. Sternberg's data was consistent with the successive (or serial) search.

Sternberg found two additional properties that were interesting. First, reaction times grew linearly with increases in memory set size. For each additional item in the memory set, subjects took (on average) an additional 38 milliseconds to make their responses. Thus, it seems the probe item is compared one-by-one with each item in STM, and each comparison takes approximately 38 milliseconds.

Second, when he compared reaction times for probe "Present" and "Absent" trials (probe item was in the memory set or not, respectively), Sternberg found no differences in reaction times. This finding is notable because an "Absent" response can only be made after *all* items in STM have been searched and found not to match the probe item. At first glance, it might seem that a "Present" trial could terminate as soon as the probe item is matched with the appropriate item in STM. As a result, with a *self-terminating* search, one would expect "Present" trials to be faster, but the data contradict this hypothesis.

The counterintuitive finding from Sternberg's study is that search of STM is always *exhaustive*. That is, the cognitive processes responsible for searching STM for a particular item search through *all* items in STM before reporting whether the probe item is in memory or not.

Sternberg's study and his analysis of the data had a major influence on models of memory and cognitive psychology in general. While more recent modeling approaches have shown that the implications of the data on theories of memory search are not as straightforward as once believed, the experimental approach and theorizing is classic. (For a review of the field, see Van Zandt and Townsend (1993).) This experiment allows you to participate in a variation of the Sternberg memory search task.

Instructions

An experiment window will appear, and a smaller window will appear with abbreviated instructions. Close the instructions window. You can open it again later from the *CogLab Info.* menu.

Start a trial by pressing the *space* bar. A fixation point will appear in the middle of the screen. After a second, a memory set consisting of 1, 3, or 5 numbers will appear on the screen for 1.2, 3.6, or 6 seconds, respectively. Study the numbers and commit them to memory. The memory set will disappear and then a probe item will appear 1 to 3 seconds later. Your task is to determine whether the probe item was in the list of just presented numbers. Respond as quickly as possible by pressing the / key (for "Present") or z key (for "Absent"). You will receive feedback on whether you were correct. When you are ready for the next trial, press the *space* bar again.

There are a minimum of 60 trials in the experimental session. For each "Present" and "Absent" condition, 10 trials are presented for each memory set size. If you make a mistake (e.g., say the item was present when it was not), the trial will be repeated (with different numbers) later in the experiment. In this way, only reaction times for trials in which you were correct are used. If you find you are often making mistakes, you should try slowing down your responses and/or try harder.

If you are distracted during a trial (e.g., you sneezed, attention drifted, you "zoned out,"...), press the *t* key instead of *z* or /. This will discard the trial. Press the *space* bar to start the next trial. The discarded trial will be rerun later in the experiment.

At the end of the experiment, the experiment window will close and a new window will appear that displays your data as a table and a plot (if appropriate) and provides an explanation of the experiment and results. You can print this information, save it as an html file, or save it in CogLab format. The latter format can be re-opened with CogLab on a CD and by your instructor who may want to combine data from students in your class.

Additional References

Houlihan, M., Pritchard, W., & Robinson, J. (2001). Effects of smoking/nicotine on performance and event-related potentials during a short-term memory scanning task. *Psychopharmacology, 156*, 388-396.

Scheffers, M., Humphrey, D., Stanny, R., Kramer, A., & Coles, M. (1999). Error-related processing during a period of extended wakefulness. *Psychophysiology, 36*, 149-157.

Kotchoubey, B., Jordan, J., Grozinger, B., Westphal, K., & Kornhuber, H. (1996). Event-related brain potentials in a varied-set memory search task: A reconsideration. *Psychophysiology, 33*, 530-540.

Basic Questions

1. What is the relationship between memory set size and reaction-time in a typical Sternberg Search task?

2. What is a self-terminating search? What is an exhaustive search?

3. Is your personal data consistent with Sternberg's findings? Explain.

Advanced Questions

1. Does your data support an exhaustive STM memory search or a self-terminating STM search? Why?

2. Use your data to predict your reaction-time for a memory set of seven items for a probe present and a probe absent response.

3. What does it mean to say there is a linear relationship between two variables? Would you classify the relationship between memory set and reaction-time from your personal data as linear?

Discussion Question

1. Do you think it is to our advantage that we use an exhaustive search of short-term memory as opposed to a self-terminating search? Why or why not?

Irrelevant Speech Effect

Minimum time to complete this experiment: 20 minutes

Background

When people are asked to recall a list of items, their performance is usually worse when the presentation of the list is accompanied by irrelevant speech. The speech does not need to be in a language that the subject knows, and doesn't even have to be real speech. Nonsense speech (such as "ba da ga") works just as well.

One reason that this phenomenon, known as the irrelevant speech effect, has attracted a lot of attention is because it seems strange that auditory information (the irrelevant speech stimuli) would interfere with visual information (the items you are trying to remember).

Although there is still no generally agreed upon explanation for this effect, there are at least three different explanations (Neath, 2000). One theory attributes the disruption to interference in working memory. The visual items are translated into a phonological code that is stored in the same part of memory (the phonological store) as the irrelevant speech. Another attributes the effect to a disruption of order information. You remember the items, but it is information about the order that is lost. A third attributes the effect to a combination of two factors, an attentional component and an interference component.

Instructions

This experiment requires a computer that can play sounds. We recommend using headphones so that you do not disturb other people. Please make sure the volume is not too loud before you put the headphones on.

An experiment window will appear, and a second smaller window will appear with abbreviated instructions. Close the instructions window. You can open it again later from the *CogLab Info.* menu.

Click on the "Next trial" button to start a trial.

On each trial, you will see a sequence of digits presented in random order. Then you will see the response buttons become active. Your task is to click on the buttons *in the same order* that the digits were presented. After you have finished clicking on all the buttons to recreate the list, click on "Next trial" to start the next sequence.

The experiment includes two types of trials: Some trials are presented with irrelevant speech (a passage from Franz Kafka in German) and some are presented with no irrelevant speech. The order of the conditions is random.

Being correct means that you click on the buttons in the same order the items appeared in the sequence. There is no way to correct mistakes in button presses, so be careful in your selections. There are 30 trials.

At the end of the experiment, the experiment window will close and a new window will appear that displays your data as a table and a plot (if appropriate) and provides an explanation of the experiment and results. You can print this information, save it as an html file, or save it in CogLab format. The latter format can be re-opened with CogLab on a CD and by your instructor who may want to combine data from students in your class.

Additional References

Toppino, T., & Pisegna, A. (2005). Articulatory suppression and the irrelevant-speech effect in short-term memory: Does the locus of suppression matter? *Psychonomic Bulletin & Review, 12*, 374-379.

Neeley, C., & LeCompte, D. (1999). The importance of semantic similarity to the irrelevant speech effect. *Memory & Cognition, 27*, 37-44.

LeCompte, D., Neely, C., & Wilson, J. (1997). Irrelevant speech and irrelevant tones: The relative importance of speech to the irrelevant speech effect. *Journal of Experimental Psychology: Learning, Memory, and Cognition, 23*, 472-483.

Basic Questions

1. In this demonstration, did you show the Irrelevant Speech Effect? Explain how you know.

2. How is visual information stored in working memory, and how might this explain the Irrelevant Speech Effect?

3. Irrelevant Speech is thought to impair one's ability to recall list items and/or impair one's ability to recall list items in the correct order. Based on your experience with this demonstration, which of these two hypotheses do you think is most accurate? Why?

Advanced Questions

1. You have an important exam tomorrow and your roommates ask you if they can have people over for a small party. They promise that you can have the whole upstairs to yourself so no one will bother you. Will this allow you to effectively study for your exam? Why or why not?

2. If you get a phone call while watching television, you always make a point to mute the television. You have always thought this allowed you to hear the person you were talking to more clearly. After having done this demonstration, can you think of another reason why muting the television allows you to communicate on the phone more effectively?

3. In this demonstration, if you were presented with auditory tones instead of irrelevant speech when being shown the sequence of numbers, do you think your recall performance would be improved, further impaired, or the same? Why?

Discussion Question

1. How might attention play a role in the Irrelevant Speech Effect?

Memory Span

Minimum time to complete this experiment: 15 minutes

Background

Many theories of cognition propose that there is a short-term or working memory system that is able to hold a limited amount of information for a short period of time. The memory span experiment is one measure of working memory capacity. In this experiment, participants are given a list of items and asked to recall the list. The list length is varied to see at what list length participants will make make few errors. That list length is the memory span for that subject on that task. Individuals with larger memory spans can better keep in mind different stimuli, and this seems to give them an advantage for a wide variety of cognitive tasks. Memory span has been linked to performance on intelligence tests, standardized tests, reading skills, problem solving, and a variety of other cognitive tasks.

The very existence of short-term memory is largely based on memory span types of experiments, as it was noted that memory span was approximately seven (plus or minus two) for a wide variety of stimuli. This suggested a simple storage system that held approximately seven items. Later studies demonstrated that memory span could be systematically influenced by a variety of stimulus characteristics. For example, when the stimuli are letters that sound alike (e.g., d, b, p, t) memory span is shorter. Likewise, memory span is shorter for lists of long words (e.g., encyclopedia, refrigerator) than for lists of short words (e.g., book, stove). These findings have suggested that the capacity of short-term memory is controlled by verbal processes. This experiment allows you to measure your memory span for a variety of stimulus types.

Instructions

An experiment window will appear, and a smaller window will appear with abbreviated instructions. Close the instructions window. You can open it again later from the *CogLab Info.* menu.

Start a trial by clicking the "Next trial" button. On the left of the window, a sequence of items will appear, with each item presented for one second. After the full sequence has been presented, the buttons on the right will show labels for item names, including those just shown. Your task is to click on the buttons just shown in the same order that the items were presented. After you have finished clicking on all the buttons to recreate the list, click on "Next trial" to start the next sequence.

The experiment includes five types of stimuli: numbers, letters that sound different, letters that sound the same, short words, and long words. In each case your task is simply to report the items you saw, in the order they were presented. Each stimulus type will be presented five times, with varying list lengths.

List length is varied, for each type of stimuli, in order to find the longest list for which you can correctly recreate the sequence. Being correct means that you both recall all the items in the sequence and click on the buttons in the same order the items appeared in the sequence. Any mistake (recalling too many items, recalling too few items, or recalling items in the wrong order) counts as Incorrect. There is no way to correct mistakes in button presses, so be careful in your selections. After clicking on "Next trial", you will be given feedback on your response to the previous sequence (Correct/Incorrect) before the next sequence is presented.

If you are correct for a given sequence, the next sequence for that stimulus type will be one item longer. If you are incorrect, the next sequence for that stimulus type will be one item shorter. In this way, the length of the sequence converges on the longest list length that you can reliably report back.

At the end of the experiment, the experiment window will close and a new window will appear that displays your data as a table and a plot (if appropriate) and provides an explanation of the experiment and results. You can print this information, save it as an html file, or save it in CogLab format. The latter format can be re-opened with CogLab on a CD and by your instructor who may want to combine data from students in your class.

Additional References

Kawai, N., & Matsuzawa, T. (2000). Numerical memory span in a chimpanzee. *Nature, 403*, 39-40.

May, C., Hasher, L., & Kane, M. (1999). The role of interference in memory span. *Memory & Cognition, 27*, 759-767.

Baddeley, A. (1994). The magical number seven: Still magic after all these years? *Psychological Review, 101*, 353-356.

Basic Questions

1. For which type of stimuli was your memory span the longest? For which was it the shortest?

2. What three types of mistakes could one make in recalling the stimulus sequence that would lead to it being scored as incorrect?

3. Approximately how many items can the average person hold in short-term memory?

Advanced Questions

1. Typically, when the stimulus sequence consists of long words, one's memory span is shorter than when the stimulus sequence consists of short words. Why might this be the case?

2. Typically, when the stimulus sequence consists of similar sounding letters, one's memory span is shorter than when the stimulus sequence consists of dissimilar sounding letters. Why might this be the case?

3. You have a friend who is taking Biology, Anatomy and Physiology, Comparative Politics, and American Government and he/she has tests in all of these classes on the same day, this upcoming Friday. Your friend decided to study for two of the exams on Wednesday and two of the exams on Thursday. Based on what you have learned about memory span, which classes would you advise him/her to study for on each of these days? Why?

Discussion Question

1. Memory span has been linked to intelligence. Suppose two individuals from different parts of the world were given the same memory test (in their respective native languages) and one individual showed a much longer memory span than the other. Using what you have learned from this demonstration, why is it unfair to say that the individual with the longer memory span is most likely more intelligent than the individual with the shorter memory span?

Operation Span

Minimum time to complete this experiment: 15 minutes

Background

Recent conceptions of memory have suggested that memory consists of a flexible workspace that not only stores information but also plays an active role in processing and manipulating information. This active process, however, seems to have a limited amount of resources to work with. One question that has been posed is whether the capacity is specific to verbal tasks or if there is a general pool of resources that is used in every working memory task. Most previous researchers have used only verbal materials in measuring working memory capacity.

To determine whether there is a general capacity for all working memory tasks, Turner and Engle (1989) developed a task called "operation-word-span" (OSPAN). In this task, subjects are asked to read and verify a simple math problem (such as (4/2)-1=1) and then read a word after the operation (such as SNOW). After a series of problems and words has been presented, the subjects recall the words that followed each operation. The number of operation-word strings in a sequence is increased and decreased to measure the subject's operation span. Operation span measures predict verbal abilities and reading comprehension even though the subjects are solving mathematical problems. Engle and his colleagues have argued that this implies a general pool of resources that is used in every type of working memory situation.

This demonstration allows you to measure your operation span using the procedure of Conway & Engle (1996).

Instructions

An experiment window will appear, and a smaller window will appear with abbreviated instructions. Close the instructions window. You can open it again later from the *CogLab Info.* menu.

Start a trial by clicking the "Next trial" button. You will see a question involving a math problem, such as:

Is 10/2 + 2 = 7 ?

Read the math problem out loud (i.e., say "Is ten divided by two plus two equal to seven?") and then decide whether the given answer is correct or incorrect. If the problem is correct, click once on the Yes button; if the problem is incorrect, click once on the No button.

You will then see a word. Read the word out loud. You will then see another math problem.

At some point, you will be asked to recall all the words from the series. Simply click on the buttons that are labeled with words you have just seen in the order in which you saw the words.

Your operation span score is valid only if you were more than 85% accurate in evaluating the math problems.

At the end of the experiment, the experiment window will close and a new window will appear that displays your data as a table and a plot (if appropriate) and provides an explanation of the experiment and results. You can print this information, save it as an html file, or save it in CogLab format. The latter format can be re-opened with CogLab on a CD and by your instructor who may want to combine data from students in your class.

Additional References

Conway, A., Kane, M., Bunting, M., Hambrick, D., Wilhelm, O., & Engle, R. (2005). Working memory span tasks: A methodological review and user's guide. *Psychonomic Bulletin & Review, 12*, 769-786.

Hitch, G., Towse, J., & Hutton, U. (2001). What limits children's working memory span? Theoretical accounts and applications for scholastic development. *Journal of Experimental Psychology: General, 130*, 184-198.

Towse, J., Hitch, G., & Hutton, U. (2000) On the interpretation of working memory span in adults. *Memory & Cognition, 28*, 341-348.

Basic Questions

1. Operation span correlates with other tasks involving working memory. What does in mean if two variables have a positive correlation? What does in mean if they have a negative correlation?

2. How is operation span calculated in this demonstration?

3. How is operation span different from what is typically described as memory span?

Advanced Questions

1. Operation-span experiments provide evidence that we have a general pool of resources for working memory. What implications does this have for multi-tasking?

2. While you are driving, your roommate reads you a list of items you need to get at the store. Why might it be difficult for you to effectively remember these items?

3. Name a job that would require someone with a high operation span. Explain your answer.

Discussion Question

1. In this demonstration, the math problems typically impair one's ability to remember the list words. Why do you think this is the case?

Phonological Similarity Effect

Minimum time to complete this experiment: 20 minutes

Background

When people are asked to recall a list of items, their performance is usually worse when the items sound similar than when the items sound different (Conrad, 1964). Although this effect has become known as the phonological similarity effect, a better term is the acoustic similarity effect because what matters is that the items sound similar to each other.

What is most surprising about the phonological similarity effect is that it occurs even when there is no auditory input, such as when you read the items silently to yourself. This result has been seen as suggesting that when reading visual items people recode the information in something like an auditory representation. If you used only a visual representation, you would be more likely to confuse items that looked similar (e.g., E and F). This idea is central to Baddeley's (1986) conception of the phonological loop, one of the components of working memory. The phonological loop has two parts: the phonological store and the articulatory control process. The phonological store is a memory store that can retain speech-based (phonological) information for a short period of time. Unless rehearsed, the traces within the store are assumed to fade and decay within about 2 seconds, after which they are no longer usable. The second component is the articulatory control process, which is responsible for two different functions: It translates visual information into a speech-based code and deposits it in the phonological store; and it refreshes a trace in the phonological store, offsetting the decay process.

According to the phonological loop model, the reason that you get a phonological similarity effect when there is no auditory input is that the articulatory control process has converted the visual information into phonological form. One key prediction is that if you somehow prevent the articulatory control process from converting the information, the phonological similarity effect will be removed. In other words, recall of similar sounding and dissimilar sounding items will be equivalent. One way of preventing this recoding is to keep the articulatory control process busy doing something else.

This demonstration is based on an experiment reported by Murray (1968) and uses a technique called articulatory suppression to prevent the articulatory control process from recoding the visual information into phonological information. On half of the trials, you will see similar sounding letters and on the other half of the trials you will see dissimilar sounding letters. On some trials, you will be asked to say "One, two, three, four, one, two, three, four, ..." out loud, over and over. You should start speaking when told to start, and you should continue until you see the response buttons become active.

78

Instructions

An experiment window will appear, and a smaller window will appear with abbreviated instructions. Close the instructions window. You can open it again later from the *CogLab Info.* menu.

Start a trial by clicking once on the 'Next trial' button. On the left of the window, a sequence of letters will appear, with each letter presented for one second. After the full sequence has been presented, the buttons on the right will show labels for the letters, including those just shown. Your task is to click on the buttons in the same order that the letters were presented. After you have finished clicking on all the buttons to recreate the list, click on Next trial to start the next sequence.

Being correct means that you both recall all the items in the sequence and click on the buttons in the same order the items appeared in the sequence. Any mistake (recalling too many items, recalling too few items, or recalling items in the wrong order) counts as Incorrect. There is no way to correct mistakes in button presses, so be careful in your selections.

On some trials, you will see the instruction "Speak" appear before the letters. You should repeatedly say "One, Two, Three, Four, One, Two, Three, Four, ..." out loud until you see the response buttons become active. You do not need to speak loudly, but you should try to speak quickly. (You should avoid doing this lab in a public space so that you do not disturb other people around you.) If you see the word "Quiet", do not say anything out loud.

The experiment includes 32 trials. Half of the trials involve articulatory suppression, and half of the trails do not. Half of the trials have letters that sound similar to each other and half of the trials have letters that all sound different.

At the end of the experiment, the experiment window will close and a new window will appear that displays your data as a table and a plot (if appropriate) and provides an explanation of the experiment and results. You can print this information, save it as an html file, or save it in CogLab format. The latter format can be re-opened with CogLab on a CD and by your instructor who may want to combine data from students in your class.

Additional References

Gupta, P., Lipinski, J., & Aktunc, E. (2005). Reexamining the phonological similarity effect in immediate serial recall: The roles of type of similarity, category cuing, and item recall. *Memory & Cognition, 33,* 1001-1016.

Li, X., Schweickert, R., & Gandour, J. (2000). The phonological similarity effect in immediate recall: Positions of shared phonemes. *Memory & Cognition, 28,* 1116-1125.

Nairne, J., & Kelley, M. (1999). Reversing the phonological similarity effect. *Memory & Cognition, 27,* 45-53.

Saito, S. (1993). Phonological similarity effect is abolished by a silent mouthing task. *Perceptual and Motor Skills, 76,* 427-431.

Basic Questions

1. In the phonological loop model, what is the phonological store?

2. What is the purpose of saying numbers aloud on half of the trials in this demonstration?

3. Did you show the phonological similarity effect? Explain.

Advanced Questions

1. Would it be harder to recall the word sequence of house, mouse, and spouse or the word sequence house, cabin, and mansion? Why?

2. In this demonstration, on half of the trials you were asked to count to four aloud over and over throughout the presentation of the sequence of letters. What other tasks could have taken the place of the counting task?

3. Using your trial-by-trial data, evaluate the types of errors you made on your first 10 trials. How many times did you fail to report a letter from the original list? How many times did you make an error in the order that you recalled the letters? Where did most of your errors occur (beginning, middle, or end of the list)?

Discussion Question

1. In a demonstration similar to this one, do you think you would be more likely to report seeing an item not on the original list in the similar quiet condition or in the dissimilar quiet condition? Explain.

Encoding Specificity

Minimum time to complete this experiment: 30 minutes

Background

According to the encoding specificity principle (Tulving, 1983) the recollection of an event depends on the interaction between the properties of the encoded event and the properties of the encoded retrieval information. In other words, whether an item will be remembered at a particular time depends on the interaction between the processing that occurred during encoding and the processing that occurred at retrieval.

This principle has important implications for what you can say about memory. Because it is the interaction of both encoding and retrieval that is important, it means that you cannot make any statement about the mnemonic properties of an item or a type of processing or a cue unless you specify both the encoding and the retrieval conditions (Tulving, 1983). Thus, you cannot say things like:

- Recognition is easier than recall.
- Deep processing is better than shallow processing.
- Pictures are recalled better than words.

These statements are all meaningless because the encoding and retrieval conditions are not mentioned. It is easy to create situations in which recall is easier than recognition, shallow processing leads to better memory than deep processing, and words are recalled better than pictures.

This demo is loosely based on Thomson and Tulving (1970). Some target words will be presented alone at study and some will be presented along with a cue. At test, there are three cue conditions: no cue, same cue, or different cue. What determines your ability to recall a particular target is the interaction between how you processed it at encoding and how you process it at test. If the cue changes, then it is likely that you will process the item in a slightly different way than when the same cue is presented again.

Instructions

A window will appear that fills nearly the entire screen, and a smaller window will appear with abbreviated instructions. Close the instructions window. You can open it again later from the *CogLab Info.* menu.

There are two phases to this demonstration. **Phase I**. Start a trial by pressing the space bar. You will see a series of word pairs, such as cup-DESK. Each pair is shown for about 3 seconds. Sometimes there won't be a cue, and instead you'll see something like ????-DESK. There are 45 pairs of words.

In **Phase II**, you will be asked to recall the words that were shown in uppercase in Phase

I. Sometimes you will be given a cue, and sometimes you won't. For example, you might see: cup-D--K. To respond, type in the two missing letters. If you can't remember the target, just type in any two letters. Press the space bar for the next test item.

There are 45 word pairs in Phase I, and 45 trials in Phase II.

At the end of the experiment, the experiment window will close and a new window will appear that displays your data as a table and a plot (if appropriate) and provides an explanation of the experiment and results. You can print this information, save it as an html file, or save it in CogLab format. The latter format can be re-opened with CogLab on a CD and by your instructor who may want to combine data from students in your class.

Additional References

Hannon, B., & Craik, F. (2001). Encoding specificity revisited: The role of semantics. *Canadian Journal of Experimental Psychology, 55,* 231-243.

Reddy, B., & Bellezza, F. (1983). Encoding specificity in free recall. *Journal of Experimental Psychology: Learning, Memory, and Cognition, 9,* 167-174.

Krane, R., & Hatton, L. (1980). Encoding specificity and modality effects in episodic memory. *Psychological Research, 42,* 353-362.

Basic Questions

1. Which cells in the data table are important for identifying an encoding specificity effect?

2. According to the encoding specificity principle, what is the most important factor for recall?

3. Do cues always help memory study and recall? Explain your answer.

Advanced Questions

1. To get a driver's license, one usually must pass a written exam as well as an in-car driving test. From what you know about encoding specificity, why is the in-car test so important?

2. You have a friend who is taking a physics course at 8am and is performing poorly on the exams. He/she tells you that he/she has been studying for the class almost every evening, but still is not performing well. Using the information your friend has given you and what you know about encoding specificity, what advice would you give your friend?

3. On Sunday morning you see someone at brunch when you recognize but you can't think of his/her name or where you know him/her from. The next day at work you see the same person again, but this time you know his/her name right away. Why might this be?

Discussion Questions

1. Using the findings surrounding encoding specificity, what suggestions about study habits would you give someone who wanted to improve his/her performance on tests?

2. You have lost your keys. What can you do to help yourself remember where you might have left them?

Levels of Processing

Minimum time to complete this experiment: 30 minutes

Background

In the 1960s, the most common view of memory was that it consisted of a series of memory stores, including sensory memory, short-term memory, and long-term memory. Beginning in the 1970s, a different perspective was developed that said that the type of processing might be more important than the hypothetical store that retained the information.

Craik and Lockhart (1972) stressed four points in the development of their Levels of Processing framework.

First, they said that memory was the result of a successive series of analyses, each at a deeper level than the previous one. A shallow level of processing could be focusing on how a word sounds; a deeper level of processing could be focusing on the meaning of a word.

Second, Craik and Lockhart assumed that the deeper the level of processing, the more durable the resulting memory. Third, the levels of processing view assumes that rehearsal can be relatively unimportant. A lot of rehearsal using a shallow level of processing will lead to worse memory than much less rehearsal using a deep level of processing.

The final point had to do with how memory should be studied: Because the emphasis is on processing rather than on structure, Craik and Lockhart suggested that researchers should use incidental learning rather than intentional learning. The reason is that the experimenter wants to study the effects of a particular type of processing. If the subject knows that there will be a memory test and tries to learn the material, the subject might use a different type of processing. If the subject is unaware that there will be a memory test, there is no reason to use a different type of processing.

	Sensory Register	Short-Term Store	Long-Term Store
Format	Literal Copy	Acoustic	Semantic
Capacity	Small	Very Small	Infinite
Duration	Up to 500 ms	Up to 30 sec	Years

There are two ways of accounting for basic memory phenomena. Reading down the table shows the structural view: If an item is in short-term store, its format will be acoustic, the capacity will be very small, and you'll be able to remember it for 20 to 30 seconds. Omitting the top row shows the processing view: If an item is encoded acoustically, the capacity is very small and the duration is around 30 seconds. According to the processing view, the first row becomes irrelevant.
Adapted from Table 5.1 of Neath & Surprenant (2003).

The typical levels of processing experiment uses incidental learning. A subject is asked to rate words based on the number of letters or consonants, or on the words' pleasantness. Because the subject is unaware that there will be a memory test later, the experimenter can assume that once the rating task is over, the subject will not process the item further. After all the ratings are done, the subject receives a surprise recall or recognition test. The usual finding is that the deeper the level of processing, the better the performance on the test.

This demonstration is adapted from one reported by Craik and Tulving (1975). Ideally, you would be unaware that there will be a memory test at the end and unaware that the three tasks are designed to induce different levels of processing.

Instructions

A window will appear that fills nearly the entire screen, and a smaller window will appear with abbreviated instructions. Close the instructions window. You can open it again later from the *CogLab Info.* menu.

Press the space bar to start each trial. There are two phases. In **Phase I**, you will see a word and a judgment task. There are three types of judgment tasks. For all judgments, you should press the *z* key to indicate a NO response and the */* key to indicate a YES response.

Judgment 1 The first type of judgment is to deicide if the word has a particular pattern of consonants and vowels. If it has the same pattern, press the */* key. If it does not, press the *z* key. For example, you might see the word *dog* followed by *cvc*. You should press the */* key because dog is spelled with a consonant, then a vowel, and then a consonant.

Judgment 2 The second type of judgment is to decide if two words rhyme. If they do, press the */* key. If they don't, press the *z* key. For example, you might see the word *fish* followed by *boat*. You should press the *z* key because they do not rhyme.

Judgment 3 The third type of judgment is to decide if one word is a synonym for another. If they do, press the */* key. If they don't, press the *z* key. For example, you might see the word *angry* followed by *mad*. You should press the */* key because both angry and mad have similar meanings.

After you have completed the judgment, press the space bar for the next trial.

After you have completed all 60 judgments, you'll enter **Phase II**. Again, you'll press the space bar to start each trial. You will be shown a series of words, half of which were shown in Phase I, and half of which are new words. You will be asked, "Was this word in Phase I?" If it was, press the */* key to indicate that YES, the word was in Phase I. It is was not, press the *z* key to indicate that NO, the word was not in Phase I. There are 60 judgments in Phase I, and 120 trials in Phase II.

At the end of the experiment, the experiment window will close and a new window will appear that displays your data as a table and a plot (if appropriate) and provides an explanation of the experiment and results. You can print this information, save it as an html file, or save it in CogLab format. The latter format can be re-opened with CogLab on a CD and by your instructor who may want to combine data from students in your class.

Additional Resources

Kronlund, A. & Whittlesea, B. (2005). Seeing double: Levels of processing can cause false memory. *Canadian Journal of Experimental Psychology, 59*, 11-16.

Royet, J., Koenig, O., Paugam-Moisy, H., Puzenat, D., & Chasse, J. (2004). Levels-of-processing effects on a task of olfactory naming. *Perceptual and Motor Skills, 98*, 197-213.

Eich, J. (1985). Levels of processing, encoding specificity, elaboration, and CHARM. *Psychological Review, 92*, 1-38.

Basic Questions

1. In this demonstration, how are you asked to evaluate words to induce a shallow level of processing? How are you asked to evaluate words to induce a deep level of processing?

2. What is incidental learning? How do researchers typically study incidental learning?

3. Was your recall performance affected by your level of processing at study? Explain.

Advanced Questions

1. A friend reads you a phone number to put in your cell phone's phonebook. Approximately how long do you have to put this number into your phonebook before you forget it?

2. Suppose you slept in on Saturday, read a book, drove to your parents' house, made your parents dinner, ate, drove home, and went to bed. On Monday, according to levels of processing theory, are you more likely to remember if you were stopped by a traffic light on your way to your parents' house or what you had for dinner? Why?

3. What methods, other than the one used in this demonstration, could be used to induce a deep level of processing for a given word?

Discussion Question

1. Describe a situation in which a shallow level of processing might be preferred over a deeper level of processing.

Serial Position

Minimum time to complete this experiment: 20 minutes

Background

This demonstration explores the effect of list position on free recall. In many instances, we are presented with a list of items and must remember each of the items (e.g., grocery lists). If the order of the items is not required for accurate recall, the task is said to be unordered or "free."

A general finding of free recall tasks is that recall of an item is strongly influenced by its position in a list. A common finding is that the last few items in the list are remembered best (called a *recency* effect), the first few items are remembered fairly well (called a *primacy* effect), but items in the middle of the list are not recalled very well at all. Surprisingly, this property holds true for many types of items and for a wide variety of memory durations (seconds to years). The effect of serial position has played a major role in the development of memory theories.

Instructions

An experiment window will appear, and a smaller window will appear with abbreviated instructions. Close the instructions window. You can open it again later from the *CogLab Info.* menu.

Start a trial by clicking the *Next trial* button. The empty space on the left of the window will show a sequence of ten letters, each presented for one second. After the full sequence has been presented, the buttons on the right will become activated. Your task is to click on the buttons that correspond to the letters in the sequence just shown *in any order*. You cannot click on more than ten buttons, and each button can be clicked only once for a given sequence. After you have finished clicking on all the buttons, click on *Next trial* to start the next sequence. The experiment includes fifteen sequences, with different letters making up the sequence each time.

Feel free to use whatever mental tricks you find helpful for recalling the consonants. Some people mentally (or verbally) rehearse items to themselves. Some people also click on the buttons for the last few items in the list before they fade from memory.

You can also create variations of this experiment by changing what you do during presentation of the sequence, or how you report back items. For example, if you try to recall the letters in the sequence in the order they were presented, you will likely find that the recency effect disappears. If you repeat a phrase to yourself during presentation of the sequence, you will likely find that your overall performance drops.

At the end of the experiment, the experiment window will close and a new window will appear that displays your data as a table and a plot (if appropriate) and provides an explanation of the experiment and results. You can print this information, save it as an html file, or save it in CogLab format. The latter format can be re-opened with CogLab on a CD and by your instructor who may want to combine data from students in your class.

Additional References

Smyth, M., Hay, D., Hitch, G., & Horton, N. (2005). Serial position memory in the visual-spatial domain: Reconstructing sequences of unfamiliar faces. *Quarterly Journal of Experimental Psychology A: Human Experimental Psychology, 58*, 909-930.

Haberlandt, K., Lawrence, H., Krohn, T., Bower, K., & Thomas, J. (2005). Pauses and durations exhibit a serial position effect. *Psychonomic Bulletin & Review, 12*, 152-158.

Surprenant, A. (2001). Distinctiveness and serial position effects in tonal sequences. *Perception & Psychophysics, 63*, 737-745.

Reed, P. (2000). Serial position effects in recognition memory for odors. *Journal of Experimental Psychology: Learning, Memory, and Cognition, 26*, 411-422.

Basic Questions

1. What is the primacy effect? Does your data show a primacy effect? Why or why not?

2. What is the recency effect? Does your data show a recency effect? Why or why not?

3. Serial position experiments typically have subjects use free recall during the test phase. What is free recall in this context?

Advanced Questions

1. If this demonstration added two items at the end of the ten item list, based on the typical serial position effects, how would the longer list change your recall of the early list items (positions 1, 2, and 3), the middle list items (positions 4, 5, 6, and 7) and the late list items (positions 8, 9, and 10)?

2. A technology company is holding open interviews from 8am to 2pm this Friday. You are very interested in the job and want to make sure you are remembered by your interviewer. Using what you have learned in this demonstration, what can you do to make this happen?

3. You are putting together a presentation for your psychology class and you notice that parts of your presentation are better than others. How should you organize your presentation to leave the class with the best impression possible?

Discussion Question

1. What types of professions could utilize what we know about serial recall? For each profession you come up with, describe specifically what they could do.

Von Restorff Effect

Minimum time to complete this experiment: 20 minutes

Background

When people are trying to remember a set of items, events, or people, they often report being able to recall the information more easily and more accurately if a particular item is distinctive or stands out in some way from similar items. This type of result is usually known as the von Restorff effect, named after Hedwig von Restorff who published her results in 1933.

In the typical von Restorff experiment, you might see a list of 7 items and your task is to recall the items in their original order. In the control condition, you might see a list such as *RMSKQLF*. In the experimental condition, you might see a list such as *RMSKQLF*. The typical finding is that you would be more likely to recall the red Q than the black Q. This effect is also sometimes known as the isolation effect because the Q is isolated in the sense that it is the only item in a different color. Research has shown that you can observe the von Restorff or isolation effect when the first item in the series is the different one. This rules out explanations based on differential encoding of the item because at the time the first item is seen, it is not different.

These results are now usually interpreted in terms of distinctiveness (Neath & Surprenant, 2003): The unusual (relative to the list) item stands out from the other items.

Instructions

An experiment window will appear, and a smaller window will appear with abbreviated instructions. Close the instructions window. You can open it again later from the *CogLab Info.* menu.

Start a trial by pressing the *Next trial* button. A sequence of 10 letters will appear on the left of the window, with each item presented for one second. After the full sequence has been presented, the buttons on the right will become active.

Your task is to click on the buttons for the items that were just shown. You can click on the buttons in any order. You are allowed to make only 10 responses. After you have clicked on 10 buttons, the remaining buttons will be disabled. After you have finished clicking on all the buttons that you remember being in the sequence, click on *Next trial* to start the next sequence.

At the end of the experiment, the experiment window will close and a new window will appear that displays your data as a table and a plot (if appropriate) and provides an explanation of the experiment and results. You can print this information, save it as an html file, or save it in CogLab format. The latter format can be re-opened with CogLab on a CD and by your instructor who may want to combine data from students in your class.

Additional References

Hunt, R., & Lamb, C. (2001). What causes the isolation effect? *Journal of Experimental Psychology: Learning, Memory, and Cognition, 27*, 1359-1366.

Holmes, C., & Arbogast, R. (1979). An auditory von Restorff effect. *Journal of General Psychology, 101*, 199-204.

Deutsch, M., & Sternlicht, M. (1967). The role of "surprise" in the von Restorff effect. *Journal of General Psychology, 76*, 151-159.

Basic Questions

1. Does your personal data reveal a Von Restorff Effect? How do you know?

2. What was done in the experimental trials of this demonstration to distinguish one of the list items from the others?

3. Excluding the distinctive list item, for which two items do you show the highest recall? Why might this have been the case?

Advanced Questions

1. In this demonstration, some of the trials had one list item that stood out from the other list items because it had a feature that was unique. This item is typically remembered with a higher frequency than its matched control, and is called the Von Restorff Effect. What do you think would happen to this effect if two of the list items shared this distinctive feature instead of one?

2. You've just started a new job and on the first day you've been told you're going to meet twelve of the company's employees, one of whom is your new supervisor. Using what you've learned about the Von Restorff Effect, what can you do to make sure you remember your new supervisor's name?

3. You're a sports agent and your new client will be competing in an open tryout in front of professional scouts. Your client is a good athlete but not well known. What advice would you give to your client help him/her get noticed during the tryout?

Discussion Question

1. How might you explain the Von Restorff Effect using interference?

False Memory

Minimum time to complete this experiment: 15 minutes

Background

An important issue for theories of cognition is how well we remember things. It is important because nearly every aspect of cognition depends on memory to some degree. To understand problem solving, decision making, attention, and perception, you need to know the abilities and limits of memory. The quality of memory is important for practical reasons as well. Many significant events depend on reports from human observers. From eyewitness testimony in murder trials to arguments with a spouse about who said what, memory and memory accuracy is critical. A surprising finding is that there is no way to assess memory accuracy without objective evidence (such as a tape recording or a photograph). The vividness or confidence of the person recalling the memory is not an accurate indication of the truth of the memory. This is not to say that most memories are inaccurate. We must be pretty accurate much of the time or else living would be quite difficult. However, for those situations in which accuracy of detail is important, memories cannot be trusted, no matter how adamant the recaller is about the vividness of the memory.

This experiment demonstrates one methodology that biases people to recall things that did not occur. The memories associated with experiments of this type are often called *false memories*. The method was first used by Deese (1959) and has been extended more recently by Roediger and McDermott (1995). The task is like many other memory experiments. A sequence of words is presented (verbally or visually) and the observer must subsequently classify a set of words as either in the sequence (old) or not in the sequence (new).

What differentiates this experiment from other memory experiments is that the sequences are specially designed to bias observers to report a particular word that was not included in the list. When people report that one of these words was in the sequence but it really was not, they are having a false memory. In some cases, people will report that they vividly recall seeing (or hearing) the word, so their memories are very strong, despite their inaccuracy.

Instructions

An experiment window will appear, and a smaller window will appear with abbreviated instructions. Close the instructions window. You can open it again later from the *CogLab Info.* menu.

Start a trial by pressing the *Next trial* button. A sequence of words will appear on the left of the window, with each word presented for one and a half seconds. After the full sequence has been presented, the buttons on the right will show labels for words, including some of those just shown. The other buttons will contain distractor words. You must distinguish the old words from the new distractor words. Your task is to click on the buttons for the words that were just shown. Not all of the words in the sequence will be listed on the buttons. After you have finished clicking on all the buttons that you remember being in the sequence, click on *Next trial* to start the next sequence.

The experiment includes only six trials. For each trial, click on the word buttons that were in the sequence just presented.

At the end of the experiment, the experiment window will close and a new window will appear that displays your data as a table and a plot (if appropriate) and provides an explanation of the experiment and results. You can print this information, save it as an html file, or save it in CogLab format. The latter format can be re-opened with CogLab on a CD and by your instructor who may want to combine data from students in your class.

Additional References

Lampinen, J., Meier, C., Arnal, J., & Leding, J. (2005). Compelling untruths: Content borrowing and vivid false memories. *Journal of Experimental Psychology: Learning, Memory, and Cognition, 31*, 954-963.

Garry, M., & Wade, K. (2005). Actually, a picture is worth less than 45 words: Narratives produce more false memories than photographs do. *Psychonomic Bulletin & Review, 12*, 359-366.

Slotnick, S., & Schacter, D. (2004). A sensory signature that distinguishes true from false memories. *Nature Neuroscience, 7*, 664-672.

Dehon, H., & Bredart, S. (2004). False memories: Young and older adults think of semantic associates at the same rate, but young adults are more successful at source monitoring. *Psychology and Aging, 19*, 191-197.

Basic Questions

1. In regard to false-memory experiments, what are special distractors?

2. Did you report seeing words that were not on the original list? If so, were these inaccurately remembered words mostly normal distractors or special distractors?

3. How can one access the accuracy of someone's memory?

Advanced Questions

1. Come up with a list of 10 words that you think could create a false memory. Using this list, what particular word/words do you think could be falsely remembered?

2. You are driving your brother and sister to your aunt's house for dinner. You haven't been to her house in a while, so you ask your siblings if either of them knows the way. Your sister says she believes she knows the way. Your brother is much more confident that he knows the way and says he can visualize the last time he went to your aunt's house. The problem is they disagree on how to get there. Whom should you believe?

3. Last time you went to see your doctor, you remembered him/her wearing a stethoscope, but later found out that, because of his/her hearing impairment, your doctor does not use a stethoscope. Why might you have been mistaken?

Discussion Question

1. What kind of implications do experiments on false memory have for evaluating the validity of eyewitness accounts?

Forgot-It-All-Along Effect

Minimum time to complete this experiment: 30 minutes

Background

There has been much controversy over the issue of *recovered memories*. (For an excellent overview, see the book edited by Conway, 1997.) This is the apparent finding that people who enter psychotherapy suddenly recover memories of events that happened to them years ago, usually memories of sexual abuse. Schooler, Bendiksen, and Ambadar (1997) use the term *discovered* rather than *recovered* memories because the latter implies that the memories are of real events whereas the former is neutral on whether the memory is of a real event or not.

Schooler et al. (1997) note that there are three independent claims being made when a person in therapy discovers a memory:

- The event that is remembered is a real event.
- The event was forgotten for a period of time.
- The event is suddenly remembered.

Schooler et al. point out that these three elements are independent. For example, the event could be real and the memory could be accurate, but there might not have been a period during which the person was unaware of the event. Each of these claims can in principle be empirically evaluated.

Schooler et al. (1997) found 4 cases in which they can demonstrate objectively that (1) the original event occurred, (2) there was a period of time during which the person did not remember the event, and (3) the memory was suddenly discovered. What this demonstrates is not that all discovered memories are of real events but rather that, in at least some cases, a person can experience an event, can fail to remember that event, and then later can recall the event.

For the memory theorist, what is most interesting is the finding that, at the time of discovery, the person has the experience of currently remembering the event but also believing they had not previously remembered the event. One explanation of this failure by people to remember what they had remembered has been termed the "forgot-it-all-along" effect (Schooler et al., 1997). (The name is based on the "knew-it-all-along" effect in which subjects who were told of a particular outcome overestimated what they would have known.) The basic idea is that during the discovered memory experience, the person thinks about the episode in a different way.

This demonstration is a laboratory analog of this "forgot-it-all-along" effect that was devised by Arnold & Lindsay (2002). No one is claiming that this is exactly the same effect as when people say they had not remembered being abused earlier but now they do.

Rather, it is a demonstration that people can forget what they had remembered.

Instructions

A window will appear that fills nearly the entire screen, and a smaller window will appear with abbreviated instructions. Close the instructions window. You can open it again later from the *CogLab Info.* menu.

There are three phases in the experiment. In Phase I, you will see a list of word pairs, a cue, and a target. In Phase II, you will receive a cued-recall test. Sometimes the cue will be the same as in Phase I and sometimes it will be different. In Phase III, you will be given a memory judgment task: You will be asked if you recalled a target in the Phase II test. You should remember that you recalled an item better when the context is the same and you should forget that you recalled an item when the context is different.

During **Phase I** you will see a series of word pairs, such as cup-DESK. Each pair is shown for about 3 seconds. There are 44 pairs of words. You need only study the pairs, they will change automatically.

In **Phase II**, you will be given a cued-recall test. You will be shown a cue and will be asked to recall the word that was presented with it in Phase I. For example, you might see: cup-D--K. To respond, type in the two missing letters. If you can't remember the target, just type in any two letters. Press the space bar for the next test item.

In **Phase III** you will be shown a cue and target pair again, but this time you will be asked if you recalled the target in Phase II. Press *y* to indicate YES you do remember recalling it; press *n* to indicate that NO, you do not remember recalling it. Press the space bar for the next test item.

There are 44 word pairs in Phase I, and 44 trials in Phase II and III.

At the end of the experiment, the experiment window will close and a new window will appear that displays your data as a table and a plot (if appropriate) and provides an explanation of the experiment and results. You can print this information, save it as an html file, or save it in CogLab format. The latter format can be re-opened with CogLab on a CD and by your instructor who may want to combine data from students in your class.

Additional References

Padilla-Walker, L., & Poole, D. (2002). Memory for previous recall: A comparison of free and cued recall. *Applied Cognitive Psychology, 16*, 515-524.

Joslyn, S., Loftus, E., McNoughton, A., & Powers, J. (2001). Memory for memory. *Memory & Cognition, 29*, 789–797.

Bouton, M., Nelson, J., & Rosas, J. (1999). Stimulus generation, context change, and forgetting. *Psychological Bulletin, 125*, 171–186.

Basic Questions

1. Why did Schooler, Bendiken, & Ambadar (1997) use the term discovered memories as opposed to recovered memories?

2. Did you forget (in Phase III) that you had correctly remembered items during the test phase (Phase II)? How do you know?

3. Were your individual experimental results similar to the predicted results of this experiment? Why or why not?

Advanced Questions

1. A friend tells you he/she does not remember telling you about his/her senior prom, but you remember him/her telling you about it very clearly. What could you do to make it more likely that he/she will remember?

2. Everyone in your Latin class did poorly on the exam last week, but the instructor tells all of you that he/she would be willing to give everyone a replacement test that would cover exactly the same material if everyone thinks they can do better. One of the other students in the class comments that they could not possibly do worse the second time around. What do you think about that statement? Why?

3. Taking into account the predicted results of this experiment, what effect does context have in memory?

Discussion Question

1. Many people have discovered memories while in therapy and sometimes these memories are of a sensitive nature (i.e., abuse, violence). How do you think these memories should be handled?

Remember/Know

Minimum time to complete this experiment: 30 minutes

Background

In a typical test of recognition memory, a subject might be shown a test item and asked if it was one that was presented on a particular list. The target might be either old -- it was on the list -- or new -- it was not on the list. If the subject decides that an old test item was on the list, it is called a hit. If the subject decides that a new test item was on the list, it is called a false alarm.

A relatively recent change in testing recognition memory has been the introduction of the Remember/Know paradigm (Tulving, 1985). When subjects judge an item to be old, they are asked to make a further distinction. If they are consciously aware of some aspects of the original episode where they were exposed to the items, they should indicate that they *remember* the item. For example, they can remember a particular thought that the word triggered, or they can remember thinking it was a coincidence that this particular word followed the previous one. If they have no conscious awareness of the learning episode, they should respond that they just *know* that the item was on the list.

The distinction can be explained in another way. If you were asked, "Who was the first president of the United States?", you most likely would name George Washington. However, you probably do not consciously recollect the original episode during which you learned this information. Rather, you just *know* the answer. In contrast, consider the following statement: Abraham Lincoln's first vice-president was Hannibal Hamlin, who was born in Paris, Maine. If, later on, someone asks you, "Who was Abraham Lincoln's first vice-president?", you might answer with Hannibal Hamlin. If you were consciously aware that you first learned this fact while reading a Web page on CogLab, you would *remember* this information in the remember/know sense. Note that it is not the type of information that makes a difference. Rather, it is the presence or absence of conscious awareness of aspects of the prior experience that are important.

This demonstration replicates studies reported by Gardiner (1988) and Rajaram (1993). You will be shown a series of words and asked to generate either a synonym or a word that rhymes. Then you will be given a recognition test in which you will be asked to indicate whether you recognize the word.

Instructions

A window will appear that fills nearly the entire screen, and a smaller window will appear with abbreviated instructions. Close the instructions window. You can open it again later from the *CogLab Info.* menu.

Press the space bar to start each trial. There are two phases. You will need a blank sheet of paper and a pen for the first phase. In **Phase I**, you will see a word and an instruction.

If the instruction says *Synonym for*, write down a word that has the same meaning as the word shown. If the instruction says *Rhymes with*, write down a word that sounds the same as the target word. When you are done, press the space bar for the next item. You will need to write down your work quickly. Each item is shown for only 5 seconds.

After this, you'll enter **Phase II**. Press the space bar to start each trial. You will be shown a series of words, half of which were shown in Phase I and half of which are new words. Please answer the question, "Was this word in Phase I?" If it was, decide whether you *remember* the word or simply *know* it was on the list. Press *r* to indicate remember, and *k* to indicate know. If the word was not on the list, press the *n* key.

The judgment *remember* means that you are consciously aware of the learning episode. You can recollect some aspect of the experience, such as the word you provided as a synonym or rhyme, or the word that came before, or your thoughts about the word. If can't recollect such information, you should choose *know*.

There are 80 words shown in Phase I and 160 trials in Phase II.

At the end of the experiment, the experiment window will close and a new window will appear that displays your data as a table and a plot (if appropriate) and provides an explanation of the experiment and results. You can print this information, save it as an html file, or save it in CogLab format. The latter format can be re-opened with CogLab on a CD and by your instructor who may want to combine data from students in your class.

Additional References

Crawley, S. & French, C. (2005). Field and observer viewpoint in remember-know memories of personal childhood events. *Memory, 13*, 673-681.

Konstantinou, I. & Gardiner, J. (2005). Conscious control and memory awareness when recognizing famous faces. *Memory, 13*, 449-457.

Gardiner, J. & Java, R. (1990). Recollective experience in word and nonword recognition. *Memory & Cognition, 18*, 23-30.

Gardiner, J. (1988). Functional aspects of recollective experience. *Memory & Cognition, 16*, 309-313.

Basic Questions

1. In the context of this demonstration what does it mean to know something? Give an example of something that you know.

2. In the context of this demonstration, what does it mean to remember something? Give an example of something that you remember.

3. Did you show a levels-of-processing effect for your remember judgments? Explain your answer.

4. Did you show a levels-of-processing effect for your know judgments? Explain your answer.

Advanced Questions

1. You are putting together a school project on NASA, and you want to include personal accounts (how they felt, where they were, what they were thinking, who they were with) of people who watched the first moon landing on live television. In your search for people who can give you these accounts, do you want to look for people who know about this historic event or remember it? Why?

2. You are at the movie theatre and you see someone you recognize. Later you find out it was your 7th grade English teacher. Would you categorize your initial recognition of your teacher as knowing or remembering? Why?

3. Your little sister starts talking about a family vacation that you had gone on quite some time ago when she was only 3 years old. She swears she remembers the trip but you are skeptical. How would you go about trying to figure out if she actually remembers the trip or just knows about the trip?

Discussion Question

1. Do you think people are more confident about things they know or things they remember? Explain your answer.

Link Word

Minimum time to complete this experiment: 30 minutes

Background

The link word method (e.g., Atkinson & Raugh, 1975) is a way of associating or linking two words together. It is based on the finding that when people form an interactive image between two concepts, one item becomes an excellent cue for retrieving the second item from memory. As applied to foreign vocabulary learning, the purpose of the link word method is to learn a working vocabulary and basic grammar of a foreign language as quickly as possible. Conversational fluency in a foreign language will be achieved only by extended study and practice in the foreign country. The link word method will get you going faster than rote learning and will complement formal instruction.

Courtesy of the Phoenix Zoo, Phoenix, AZ.
Photo by Dick George.

Gruneberg (1994) describes a system for learning French. (There are systems for other languages also; see unforgettablelanguages.com.) The key is to form an interactive image made up of one object that corresponds to the English word and one that corresponds to the French. For example, the French for goat is *chèvre* (SHEVR). Imagine a goat sleeping on your Chevy truck. Carefully study the image you have formed for about 10 seconds or so. After studying about 10 words, a quick test is given. This ensures practice in generating the French word.

Then a bit of grammar is introduced. French words are either masculine (*le*) or feminine (*la*). To remember the gender of a word, you create an interactive image with either a boxer (to convey masculine) or a bottle of French perfume (to convey feminine). For example, imagine pouring a bottle of perfume over a goat to stop the bad smell. Then imagine a boxer punching a rabbit. You learn the gender of the words you previously learned, and then are tested again (e.g., you are asked to come up with *la chèvre* and *le lapin*).

The next stage is to learn about a dozen useful words, such as adjectives (which are then tested), followed by learning the French present tense of to be. Finally, you put all of this together and produce sentences such as *Le lapin est petit*. You can go through an entire

102

book in about twelve hours or so, and end up with a vocabulary of 500 or more words. More importantly, you can easily remember the words that you have learned.

This demonstration illustrates the use of the link word technique to learn words. (It won't cover grammar, etc.) The words and descriptions come from Gruneberg (1994) and are used with permission of the author, Dr. Michael Gruneberg.

Instructions

An experiment window will appear, and a smaller window will appear with instructions. Be sure to read the instructions carefully. There are two different versions of the experiment and the instructions differ across the versions. Close the instructions window. You can open it again later from the *CogLab Info.* menu.

Click once on the *Next trial* button to start a trial. You will see a French word (with a guide to pronunciation) and the word's meaning in English. Try to spend 10 seconds studying the word pair.

After you have seen 50 words, you will be given a vocabulary test. For the test, you will be shown a French word and asked to type in the English meaning. When you have entered the word, click once on the *Next trial* button.

There are 50 words, and 50 test questions for a total of 100 trials.

At the end of the experiment, the experiment window will close and a new window will appear that displays your data as a table and a plot (if appropriate) and provides an explanation of the experiment and results. You can print this information, save it as an html file, or save it in CogLab format. The latter format can be re-opened with CogLab on a CD and by your instructor who may want to combine data from students in your class.

Additional References

Beaton, A., Gruneberg, M., Hyde, C., Shufflebottom, A., & Sykes, R. (2005). Facilitation of receptive and productive foreign vocabulary learning using the keyword method: The role of image quality. *Memory, 13*, 458-471.

Campos, A., Amor, A., & Gonzalez, M. (2004). The importance of the keyword-generation method in keyword mnemonics. *Experimental Psychology, 51*, 125-131

Campos, A., Gonzalez, M., & Amor, A. (2003). Limitations of the mnemonic-keyword method. *Journal of General Psychology, 130*, 399-413.

Wieczynski, D., & Blick, K. (1996). Self-referencing versus the keyword method in learning vocabulary words. *Psychological Reports, 79*, 1391-1394.

Basic Questions

1. Look at your individual data. How many words did you correctly translate? For the words you correctly translated, did you use the image you visualized during the study phase?

2. There was no control condition in this experiment. What could have been done to add a control condition?

3. How does forming an interactive image between a concept you are not familiar with and a concept you are familiar with help with recall of the unfamiliar item?

Advanced Questions

1. Using the link word method, what types of images are most effective in helping people remember?

2. The Spanish word for dog is perro and the Spanish word for cat is gato. Use the link word method to help yourself remember how to translate perro and gato from Spanish to English. Describe your process.

3. In what other situations could one use the link word method besides learning a foreign language? For each situation you come up with, give an example of one of the images you might use.

Discussion Question

1. What problems do you foresee in using the link word method for learning a foreign language?

Mental Rotation

Minimum time to complete this experiment: 30 minutes

Background

When we carry out some cognitive tasks, we seem to use *mental images*. For example, how many windows are in your house or apartment? To answer this question, most people seem to recall a mental map of their home and, mentally, move through the map as they count windows.

Although everyone seems to experience something that we call mental imagery, it is difficult to draw conclusions from such introspections. For example, some people report that their mental images are very sketchy and ill defined, while others report their mental images are detailed and crisp. Based solely on these reports, it is impossible to know whether people's mental images really differ, or if subjects just describe the mental images differently.

To explore mental images more objectively, researchers give subjects tasks that seem to require the use of mental images. As a critical part of the task is varied, some characteristics of mental images can be deduced. Roger Shepard and his colleagues (e.g., Shepard & Metzler, 1971) designed one of the most often-used tasks. In this task, subjects were shown two novel visual stimuli and were asked to determine whether the stimuli had the same shape or different (mirror image) shapes. The shapes (random block shapes) were *rotated* around the vertical axis. Subjects reported that they mentally rotated a shape in their head until the two stimuli were oriented the same way, and then made their judgment.

When subjects were asked to make their responses as quickly as possible, the reaction time increased with the angle of rotation between the shapes. This suggests that it takes *time* to mentally rotate an image, and implies that mental images are much like real images. Shepard further found that every 50 degrees of physical rotation required one second of mental rotation before subjects could respond. This suggests that the rate of mental rotation is at a constant velocity.

Shepard's findings have had a large influence on theories of mental representation. This experiment allows you to participate in the mental rotation task.

Instructions

A window will appear that fills nearly the entire screen, and a smaller window will appear with abbreviated instructions. Close the instructions window. You can open it again later from the *CogLab Info.* menu.

Start a trial by pressing the *space* bar. Two 3-D block shapes will appear on the screen, one to the left and one to the right. Each block shape is within a circle. The two shapes are either identical, or different (one is a mirror image of the other). One shape is also rotated around the vertical axis. The rotation was 0, 20, 40, 60, 80, 100, or 120 degrees relative to the orientation of the other shape. Your task is to determine whether the two shapes are the same or not. Respond as quickly as possible by pressing the / key (for "same") or the z key (for "different"). You will receive feedback on whether you were correct. When you are ready for the next trial, press the *space* bar again.

There is a minimum of 70 trials. For each pair of "same" and "different" stimuli, five trials are presented for each rotation angle. If you make a mistake (e.g., say the stimuli are different when they were actually the same), the trial will be repeated (with different stimuli) later in the experiment. In this way, only reaction times for which you were correct are used. If you find you are often making mistakes, you should try slowing down on your responses and/or try harder.

At the end of the experiment, the experiment window will close and a new window will appear that displays your data as a table and a plot (if appropriate) and provides an explanation of the experiment and results. You can print this information, save it as an html file, or save it in CogLab format. The latter format can be re-opened with CogLab on a CD and by your instructor who may want to combine data from students in your class.

Additional References

Ginn, S., & Pickens, S. (2005). Relationships between spatial activities and scores on the mental rotation test as a function of sex. *Perceptual and Motor Skills, 100,* 877-881.

Nakatani, C., & Pollatsek, A. (2004). An eye movement analysis of "mental rotation" of simple scenes. *Perception & Psychophysics, 66,* 1227-1245.

Olivier, G., Velay, J., Labiale, G., Celse, C., & Faure, S. (2004). Mental rotation and simulation of a reaching and grasping manual movement. *Perceptual and Motor Skills, 98,* 1107-1116.

Heil, M. (2002). The functional significance of ERP effects during mental rotation. *Psychophysiology, 39,* 535-545.

Basic Questions

1. Were your personal experimental results similar to the predicted experimental results? Explain your answer.

2. Why did Shepard & Metzler's (1971) findings suggest that mental images were similar to real images?

3. In demonstrations like this, participants often report that they mentally rotate the objects in their minds in order to make their same/different judgments, so why did researches decide to take reaction-time measurements also?

Advanced Questions

1. Using your data, predict your reaction-time for making a same response if you were shown two identical shapes but one of the shapes had been rotated 140 degrees on the y-axis.

2. In this demonstration, why did you have to repeat the trial if you made an incorrect same/different judgment?

3. You are trying to get a new mattress through your front door. Currently, the mattress is laying flat on your front porch. You look at the mattress and mentally rotate the object in your mind to figure out how it might fit through the doorway. There are two ways the mattress could conceivably fit through the doorway: it could be slightly tilted to one side or it could be stood up on end. Using what you have learned in this demonstration, which of these two possibilities are you more likely to come up with first? Why?

Discussion Question

1. Describe some cognitive tasks (not already mentioned in the text) in which one might utilize mental imagery.

Categorical Perception - Identification

Minimum time to complete this experiment: 20 minutes

Background

People perceive most stimuli continuously. For example, when you look at a rainbow, you see a smooth transition from red to yellow (like the image below):

You usually do not perceive stimuli categorically. Categorical perception means that you see either pure red or pure yellow and nothing in between (like the image below):

This is called "categorical" perception because, instead of getting a percept that is ambiguous, you get a percept that perfectly matches an ideal example of a particular category. One thing that people seem to perceive categorically is speech (Harnard, 1987). What is interesting about this is that even when the physical stimuli change continuously (like the upper image), people perceive it categorically (like the lower image).

For example, both /b/ and /p/ are stop consonants: To produce these, you close your lips, then open them, release some air, and the vocal chords begin vibrating. Hold your hand in front of your mouth and say /ba/ and then /pa/. The difference between /ba/ and /pa/ is the time between the release of the air and the beginning of the vibration. This is referred to as voice onset time or VOT. For /b/, VOT is very short. Voicing begins at almost the same time as the air is released. For /p/, the voicing is delayed.

Researchers can construct a series of stimuli in which the VOT changes in small steps. When people are asked to identify these stimuli, they generally have no difficulty: The first few are identified as /b/ and the last few are identified as /p/. What is most interesting is how the middle items are identified. Unlike most other stimuli, people do not report hearing something that is a bit like /b/ and a bit like /p/. Rather, they report hearing either /b/ or /p/.

To demonstrate categorical perception of speech stimuli, you really need two different measures. This lab provides one of those measures: It lets you find the point at which your percept changes from ba to pa through an identification task. The second (which is provided in the Categorical Perception - Discrimination experiment) examines your ability to tell whether two tokens are the same or different.

Instructions

This experiment requires a computer that can play sounds. We recommend using headphones so that you do not disturb other people. Please make sure the volume is not too loud before *you put the headphones on.*

An experiment window will appear, and another window will appear with abbreviated instructions. Close the instructions window. You can open it again later from the *CogLab Info.* menu.

Click once on the Next trial button to hear a sound. Your task is to report what it most sounds like. Click once on the *BA* button if you think the sound was most like BA or click once on the *PA* button if you think the sound was most like PA.

Occasionally, the sound that is played may be distorted. If you did not hear the sound clearly, click once on the *Redo* button instead of on the *BA* or *PA* buttons. The trial will be repeated later on in the session. There are 10 trials for each stimulus, for a total of 90 trials.

At the end of the experiment, the experiment window will close and a new window will appear that displays your data as a table and a plot (if appropriate) and provides an explanation of the experiment and results. You can print this information, save it as an html file, or save it in CogLab format. The latter format can be re-opened with CogLab on a CD and by your instructor who may want to combine data from students in your class.

Additional References

Baker, S., Idsardi, W., Golinkoff, R., & Petitto, I. (2005). The perception of handshapes in American sign language. *Memory & Cognition, 33*, 887-904.

Quinn, P. (2004). Visual perception of orientation is categorical near vertical and continuous near horizontal. *Perception, 33*, 897-906.

Damper, R., & Harnad, S. (2000). Neural network models of categorical perception. *Perception & Psychophysics, 62*, 843-867.

Basic Questions

1. What is an identification task? Give an example of an identification task.

2. What aspect of speech sound is the primary factor in determining if one perceives the /ba/ sound or the /pa/ sound?

3. Did your personal data show you had a strong tendency for categorical perception? Explain your answer.

Advanced Questions

1. In this demonstration, there were nine speech sound stimulus conditions (Ba1, Ba2, … Ba9). Each stimulus condition, as displayed on the experimental results page, had a VOT that was delayed 5ms from the condition before it. Let's pretend that we also did another experiment similar to this one, except that we used 45 speech sound stimulus conditions and each condition was delayed 1ms from the condition before it. Would you predict the pattern of results to be similar to or different from those of this demonstration? Explain your answer.

2. In many situations we are forced to make categorical judgments. Name a job in which someone has to categorize people/things that actually fall on a continuum. Describe the categorization this person has to make.

3. Why is it useful for us to have categorical speech perception?

Discussion Question

1. Other than its own auditory properties, what do we use to help us identify a given speech sound?

Categorical Perception - Discrimination

Minimum time to complete this experiment: 20 minutes

Background

People perceive most stimuli continuously. For example, when you look at a rainbow, you see a smooth transition from red to yellow (like the image below):

You usually do not perceive stimuli categorically. Categorical perception means that you see either pure red or pure yellow and nothing in between (like the image below):

This is called "categorical" perception because, instead of getting a percept that is ambiguous, you get a percept that perfectly matches an ideal example of a particular category. One thing that people seem to perceive categorically is speech (Harnard, 1987). What is interesting about this is that even when the physical stimuli change continuously (like the upper image), people perceive it categorically (like the lower image).

For example, both /b/ and /p/ are stop consonants: To produce these, you close your lips, then open them, release some air, and the vocal chords begin vibrating. Hold your hand in front of your mouth and say /ba/ and then /pa/. The difference between /ba/ and /pa/ is the time between the release of the air and the beginning of the vibration. This is referred to as voice onset time or VOT. For /b/, VOT is very short. Voicing begins at almost the same time as the air is released. For /p/, the voicing is delayed.

Researchers can construct a series of stimuli in which the VOT changes in small steps. When people are asked to identify these stimuli, they generally have no difficulty: The first few are identified as /b/ and the last few are identified as /p/. What is most interesting is how the middle items are identified. Unlike most other stimuli, people do not report hearing something that is a bit like /b/ and a bit like /p/. Rather, they report hearing either /b/ or /p/.

To demonstrate categorical perception of speech stimuli, you really need two different measures. The first examines your ability to identify which sound you are hearing (and is provided in the Categorical Perception - Identification experiment). The second examines your ability to tell whether two tokens are the same or different. If you are perceiving the stimuli categorically, it should be easy for you to correctly say that the tokens are different if they come from opposite sides of the category boundary. It should be very difficult for you to decide they are different if they come from the same side of the category boundary. In this lab, you will hear two sounds and your task is to say whether they are the same or different.

Instructions

This experiment requires a computer that can play sounds. We recommend using headphones so that you do not disturb other people. Please make sure the volume is not too loud before *you put the headphones on.*

An experiment window will appear, and another window will appear with abbreviated instructions. Close the instructions window. You can open it again later from the *CogLab Info.* menu.

Click once on the "Next trial" button to hear two sounds. Your task is to report if they are the same or different. If you think they are the same, click once on the *Same* button. If you think they are different, click once on the *Different* button.

Occasionally, the sound that is played may be distorted. If you did not hear the sound clearly, click once on the *Redo* button; the trial will be repeated later on in the session. There are 140 trials.

At the end of the experiment, the experiment window will close and a new window will appear that displays your data as a table and a plot (if appropriate) and provides an explanation of the experiment and results. You can print this information, save it as an html file, or save it in CogLab format. The latter format can be re-opened with CogLab on a CD and by your instructor who may want to combine data from students in your class.

Additional References

Serniclaes, W., Ventura, P., Morais, J., & Kolinsky, R. (2005). Categorical perception of speech sounds in illiterate adults. *Cognition, 98,* B35-B44.

Laukka, P. (2005). Categorical perception of vocal emotion expressions. *Emotion, 5,* 277-295.

Gerrits, E., & Schouten, M. (2004). Categorical perception depends on the discrimination task. *Perception & Psychophysics, 66,* 363-376.

Basic Questions

1. What is a discrimination task? Give an example.

2. Did your personal experimental results follow a pattern similar to the predicted experimental results? Why or why not?

3. Define VOT (voice onset time).

Advanced Questions

1. List some other properties of speech sounds.

2. In an experiment a researcher often looks at the average performance across a group of participants rather than just looking at the performance of one individual. Why is this useful in evaluating the effects of an experiment's independent variables?

3. Variations caused by mispronunciation, environmental auditory noise, and a variety of other factors could cause one to categorize a speech sound incorrectly. Similar speech sounds are susceptible to erroneous categorization. For example, we have learned that the consonant sounds of /b/ and /p/ are similar. List some word pairs that may be confused with each other because of an incorrectly categorized /b/ or /p/ speech sound.

Discussion Question

1. Can experience and/or training affect one's ability to make perceptual discriminations? Give support for your answer.

Lexical Decision

Minimum time to complete this experiment: 15 minutes

Background

Theories of human language propose that a mental dictionary exists, a lexicon, that contains a variety of information about words. This lexicon contains information about a word's meaning (its semantic content), its part of language (noun, verb, adjective, etc.), and its relationships to other words (What can it follow? What can follow it? How can it be modified?). Psychologists are interested in the organization of this lexicon.

The lexicon is similar to a dictionary in that it holds information about words and other components of language. Physical dictionaries generally organize words alphabetically. This arrangement makes it easy to find any word, provided the spelling is known or can be guessed. Because dictionaries usually are used to find the meanings of known words or to check if a word is spelled properly, this organization is useful.

In the mental lexicon, though, the most useful feature of a word may not be its spelling, but its meaning and its relationship to other words. If words are arranged in the lexicon by semantic relationships, words that are related to each other (e.g., chair, seat, table) would be close together in the lexicon, whereas words that are unrelated to each other (e.g., chair, dinosaur, broccoli) would be far apart.

In this demonstration, you will be asked to determine if a series of letters is a word or a nonword. The computer will record your reaction time, that is, how fast you are able to make your decision about each letter string. Remember to make your decision as quickly and accurately as you can.

Instructions

A window will appear that fills nearly the entire screen, and a smaller window will appear with abbreviated instructions. Close the instructions window. You can open it again later from the *CogLab Info.* menu.

Press the space bar to start a trial. A small fixation square will appear in the middle of the screen. Fix on this square. One to four seconds later, a word or nonword will appear above the fixation square. Decide if the item is a word or a nonword as quickly as possible. Press the / key if the item is a word. Press the z key if the item is not a word. The item will disappear when you press either of these keys, so you will know your response has been recorded.

Two to three seconds later, the next word or nonword will appear. Again, decide if the item is a word or nonword by pressing the / key or z key as quickly as possible. You will receive feedback when you respond too quickly (before the item appears), too slowly, or incorrectly.

There are at least 70 total trials. You must classify the items correctly for the trial to count, so if you find that you are making many classification mistakes, slow down.

At the end of the experiment, the experiment window will close and a new window will appear that displays your data as a table and a plot (if appropriate) and provides an explanation of the experiment and results. You can print this information, save it as an html file, or save it in CogLab format. The latter format can be re-opened with CogLab on a CD and by your instructor who may want to combine data from students in your class.

Additional References

Ratcliff, R., Thapar, A., Gomez, P., & McKoon, G. (2004). A diffusion model analysis of the effects of aging in the lexical-decision task. *Psychology and Aging, 19*, 278-289.

Ratcliff, R., Gomez, P., & McKoon, G. (2004). A diffusion model account of the lexical decision task. *Psychological Review, 111*, 159-182.

Chwilla, D., & Kolk, H. (2002). Three-step priming in lexical decision. *Memory & Cognition, 30*, 217-225.

Wentura, D. (2000). Dissociative affective and associative priming effects in the lexical decision task: Yes versus no responses to word targets reveal evaluative judgment tendencies. *Journal of Experimental Psychology: Learning, Memory, and Cognition, 26*, 456-469.

Basic Questions

1. What types of information are held in one's mental lexicon?

2. Were your results consistent with the demonstration predictions? Explain your answer.

3. Demonstrations like the one you just completed typically show semantic priming. What is semantic priming?

Advanced Questions

1. You enjoy watching game shows and one of your favorites is Jeopardy. Jeopardy is a quiz show in which contestants answer questions from a set of identified categories. When you watch the show, you notice that if you did not see the question category before the question was asked you are never able to come up with the correct answer before the question timer runs out. Using what you have learned from this demonstration, why might this be the case?

2. Identify words that would prime each of the following words: cold, angry, and soft.

3. You are writing a test and you want to make it as challenging as possible. Using what you have learned in this demonstration, how can you organize the test questions to achieve this goal?

Discussion Question

1. This demonstration showed semantic priming. What other types of word priming are there? Describe each one you come up with.

Word Superiority

Minimum time to complete this experiment: 30 minutes

Background

Humans are extremely good at recognizing visual patterns. Even the fastest of modern computers are nowhere near as efficient or thorough at identifying visual targets. How we acquired this level of sophistication is not fully understood. What is clear is that context plays an important role in interpreting a physical stimulus. We are not simply detectors of patterns of light; instead, we infer interpretations of the physical stimulus.

The effect of context is made clear in a phenomenon called the word superiority effect (Reicher, 1969). In the experiment, an isolated letter such as K or a word such as WORK is briefly flashed on the screen and then immediately replaced by a mask of Xs and Os. The observer is then forced to choose between whether a D or a K was presented. A key component of the experiment is that either of the choices at the end of WOR would create a valid word. Thus, the observer's knowledge that the presentation contained a word does not automatically tell him which letter was presented. Even with this control, the experimental finding is that detection of K is better when it is part of a word than when it is presented in isolation. This is the word superiority effect.

This result seems paradoxical. In detecting an isolated letter, there is only one item to focus on. When a word is presented, more letters must be processed before the word can be detected. Thus, it would seem, detecting a letter in a word should be more difficult than detecting a letter in isolation. The data, however, demonstrate exactly the opposite effect.

This finding has been of significant interest to researchers who explore the processes involved in recognizing patterns. Although the word superiority effect has been a motivating result for a variety of theories, the effect has not been completely explained by any current theory. This demonstration allows you to participate in a version of the word superiority experiment.

Instructions

A window will appear that fills nearly the entire screen, and a smaller window will appear with abbreviated instructions. Close the instructions window. You can open it again later from the *CogLab Info.* menu.

Start a trial by pressing the space bar. A fixation dot will appear in the middle of the window. Stare at it. One second later, a word or an isolated letter will briefly flash on the screen. The duration of this word or letter is very brief (approximately 40 milliseconds). Then the word/letter is replaced with a mask of Xs and Os. Half a second later, instructions will appear on which position you are to report on. These instructions are of the form *--- S or M? This indicates that you are to report on whether the letter in the first

117

position is an S or an M. An instruction such as --*- E or L? indicates that you are to report on whether the letter in the third position is an E or a L. Simply type in the letter that you saw at the indicated position. You will not receive any feedback on whether your guess was correct. The letter you type, however, will be shown in red on the bottom half of the screen. This indicates that the computer has registered the key you pressed.

You may find that in some trials you have no idea what the queried letter was. In those cases, just guess one of the options. (You may find that on the isolated letter trials you see a letter but it is in a different place than you are queried. Guessing that letter might be a good strategy because, with these brief durations, things sometimes seem to jump around.)

There are a total of 96 trials. There are 16 four letter words and 16 isolated letters in different locations. Each condition is repeated three times. If you respond before the probe appears, the trial will be repeated later. Press the space bar to start each trial.

At the end of the experiment, the experiment window will close and a new window will appear that displays your data as a table and a plot (if appropriate) and provides an explanation of the experiment and results. You can print this information, save it as an html file, or save it in CogLab format. The latter format can be re-opened with CogLab on a CD and by your instructor who may want to combine data from students in your class.

Additional References

Grainger, J., Bouttevin, S., Truc, C., Bastien, M., & Ziegler, J. (2003). Word superiority, pseudoword superiority, and learning to read: A comparison of dyslexic and normal readers. *Brain and Language, 87*, 432-440.

Salvemini, A., Stewart, A., Purcell, D., & Pinkham, R. (1998). A word-superiority effect in the presence of foveal load. *Perceptual and Motor Skills, 86*, 1311-1319.

Krueger, L. (1992). The word-superiority effect and phonological recoding. *Memory & Cognition, 20*, 685-694.

Estes, W., & Brunn, J. (1987). Discriminability and bias in the word-superiority effect. *Perception & Psychophysics, 42*, 411-422.

Basic Questions

1. What is the word superiority effect?

2. Does your data show the word superiority effect? Explain why or why not.

3. Why could one argue that the typical word superiority effect findings are counter intuitive?

Advanced Questions

1. What is bottom-up information? What is top-down information?

2. Using the definitions from your answer to Advanced Question one, which type of information is likely to be the cause of the differences in letter detection performance typically seen in the word superiority effect? Explain your answer.

3. You walk by the same art gallery everyday on your way home from work. Sometimes when walking by the gallery, you glance through the store window, but all you are able to see is that there is something painted on the back wall. You see it clearly enough to describe it very well yet you have no idea what it is. One day you decide to go inside the gallery. You find out that what you were seeing was the nose from a wall mural of a woman's face. Why were you unable to identify what you had seen until you went inside the gallery?

Discussion Question

1. We often encounter ambiguous stimuli in our environment. Describe a situation in which contextual information could be used to help identify an ambiguous stimulus. Be sure to identify the various possibilities of the stimulus, the context, and what one might conclude about the stimulus based on the contextual information.

Absolute Identification

Minimum time to complete this experiment: 15 minutes

Background

Lots of research in cognitive psychology has focused on whether there is a fundamental limit on people's capacity to process information and, if so, what that limit is. It might often seem that we have almost unlimited potential, especially when it comes to identifying and recognizing different items. Think of all the different people you can identify, or cars, or animals, or buildings, or pieces of furniture. Given the ease with which all of these items can be identified, it comes as a surprise to most people to find that when items vary in just one dimension, they cannot identify even seven items. The research that demonstrates this limitation is often done using a procedure known as absolute identification.

In a typical absolute identification experiment, people are exposed to a set of stimuli that vary systematically along only one dimension (e.g., nine tones of different frequencies, or eight lines of different lengths). A label, often a digit, is associated with each stimulus. The task is simply to produce the correct label in response to the presentation of an item from the set.

When the items are evenly spaced, the first and last items in the series are identified most easily. In contrast, identification of the middle items is usually quite poor. Such effects are found for many dimensions, such as frequency, loudness, weight, area, line length, and semantic continua.

One curious aspect is that performance seems fundamentally limited: No matter how many trials you are never perfect at this task as long as the stimuli vary along only one dimension (Shiffrin & Nosofsky, 1994). If the stimuli varied along two or more dimensions, the task becomes trivially easy. For example, you probably have no trouble identifying the letters in the alphabet. This is because the letters vary on multiple dimensions including height (the letter 't' is taller than the letter 'e'), curvature (the letter 'i' is straight, the letter 's' is all curves), and others.

Instructions

This experiment requires a computer that can play sounds. We recommend using headphones so that you do not disturb other people. Please make sure the volume is not too loud before you put the headphones on.

A window will appear that fills nearly the entire screen, and a smaller window will appear with abbreviated instructions. Close the instructions window. You can open it again later from the *CogLab Info.* menu.

Click on the space bar to start a trial. You will first hear all 9 tones. Tone 1 is the lowest

120

in pitch, tone 9 is the highest in pitch. Adjust the volume on your computer as appropriate, then press the space bar again to start the demonstration.

On each trial, you will hear one of the 9 tones. Your task is to press a key that indicates which tone you think it is. For example, if you think it is Tone 2, press the *2* key. If you think it is Tone 6, press the *6* key. The computer will tell if you were correct. If you were not correct, the computer will also tell you which tone it was. You start each trial by pressing the *space bar*. There are 90 trials. This sounds like a lot, but it takes only a couple of seconds per trial.

At the end of the experiment, the experiment window will close and a new window will appear that displays your data as a table and a plot (if appropriate) and provides an explanation of the experiment and results. You can print this information, save it as an html file, or save it in CogLab format. The latter format can be re-opened with CogLab on a CD and by your instructor who may want to combine data from students in your class.

Additional References

Stewart, N., Brown, G., & Chater, N. (2005). Absolute identification by relative judgment. *Psychological Review, 112*, 881-911.

Rouder, J., Morey, R., Cowan, N., & Pfaltz, M. (2004). Learning in a unidimensional absolute identification task. *Psychonomic Bulletin & Review, 11*, 938-944.

McCormack, T., Brown, G., Maylor, E., Richardson, L., & Darby, R. (2002). Effects of aging on absolute identification of duration. *Psychology and Aging, 17*, 363-378.

Lacouture, Y., & Lacerte, D. (1997). Stimulus modality and stimulus-response compatibility in absolute identification. *Canadian Journal of Experimental Psychology, 51*, 165-170.

Basic Questions

1. In what dimension did the tones in this demonstration vary?

2. If you were given extensive training on this task, how would your results change?

3. Which tones were you most accurately able to identify? Which tones did you have the most difficulty identifying?

Advanced Questions

1. Using your data, graph the results of this demonstration by plotting the tones presented (1-9) on the x-axis and the average number of times each tone was correctly identified on the y-axis. What is the general shape of the curve you just plotted?

2. Identify a category of items for which you are good at distinguishing among its members. Why is your identification performance of items within this category so good?

3. You are designing an interface for a control room at a factory. One of the factory employees shows you the interface they currently use. One of the features of the old interface is a light indicator that goes off multiple times a day. Its flashing rate indicates one of 7 responses that the control-room operator needs to make. Why is this aspect of the current interface design problematic? What could you do to make it better?

Discussion Question

1. In what ways are the predicted results of this demonstration similar to the typical results from an ordered serial recall task?

Implicit Learning

Minimum time to complete this experiment: 25 minutes

Background

The term *implicit learning* refers to "the process by which knowledge about the rule-governed complexities of the stimulus environment is acquired independently of conscious attempts to do so" (Reber, 1989, p. 219).

One form of implicit learning involves serial pattern learning. In this task, subjects are asked to press one of four keys as quickly as they can whenever they see a stimulus, such as an asterisk, appear in any of four locations (labeled A, B, C, and D). If the asterisk appears in location A, the subject is asked to press (for example) the 'z' key. If the asterisk appears in location B, the subject is asked to press the 'x' key. There is an underlying pattern that defines the order of locations. It is this pattern that the subject will learn. As the sequence is repeated, subjects press the keys more quickly. This indicates that learning has taken place. More evidence comes from a transfer test, in which the pattern is changed (again, without telling the subject). Now the subjects press the keys much more slowly.

The key evidence to support the idea that learning is implicit -- not conscious -- comes from tests in which subjects are asked what the pattern was. The typical finding is that subjects are unaware of the pattern, but their behavior shows that they have nonetheless learned it (see Stadler & Frensch, 1998).

This demonstration is based on a study reported by Destrebecqz and Cleeremans (2001). There will be a long series of trials in which you will be asked to indicate the location of a circle. Please try to respond as quickly as you possibly can.

Instructions

A window will appear that fills nearly the entire screen, and a smaller window will appear with abbreviated instructions. Close the instructions window. You can open it again later from the *CogLab Info.* menu.

Start a trial by pressing the space bar. A short time later, a circle will appear in one of the four locations shown below. Your task is to indicate the location of the circle by pressing the appropriate key as quickly as you can.

- If the circle appears in the left-most location, press the *z* key as quickly as you can.
- If the circle appears in the second location, press the *x* key as quickly as you can.
- If the circle appears in the third location, press the . key as quickly as you can.
- If the circle appears in the right-most location, press the / key as quickly as you can.

If the . and / keys are not the right-most keys on your keyboard, please use the *Instructions* menu (that will appear once you start the demo) to change the response keys so that you are using the right-most keys. There are 288 trials (each trial takes only a few seconds), and you can take a rest every 24 trials. Press the space bar to start each trial.

At the end of the experiment, the experiment window will close and a new window will appear that displays your data as a table and a plot (if appropriate) and provides an explanation of the experiment and results. You can print this information, save it as an html file, or save it in CogLab format. The latter format can be re-opened with CogLab on a CD and by your instructor who may want to combine data from students in your class.

Additional References

Kuhn, G., & Dienes, Z. (2005). Implicit learning of nonlocal musical rules: Implicitly learning more than chunks. *Journal of Experimental Psychology: Learning, Memory, and Cognition, 31*, 1417-1432.

Jiang, Y., & Leung, A. (2005). Implicit learning of ignored visual context. *Psychonomic Bulletin & Review, 12*, 100-106.

Karpicke, J., & Pisoni, D. (2004). Using immediate memory span to measure implicit learning. *Memory & Cognition, 32*, 956-964

Degel, J., Piper, D., & Koster, E. (2001). Implicit learning and implicit memory for odors: The influence of odor identification and retention time. *Chemical Senses, 26*, 267-280.

Basic Questions

1. What is the main difference between explicit and implicit learning?

2. While doing this demonstration did you feel as though you were learning a pattern of responses? Were you surprised to find out you participated in the version (random/pattern) of the experiment you did?

3. Using your individual data, determine if implicit learning took place? Explain why you drew the conclusion that you did.

Advanced Questions

1. You have just received you driver's license and the first place you drive to on your own is to your music lesson. When you get to your lesson, your instructor asks you what driving route you took to get there. You have a great deal of trouble describing your driving route to your instructor, but obviously you had no problem getting there. Explain how this could happen.

2. You just finished taking a mid-term exam in your hardest class of the semester. Despite it being a multiple-choice test (there were only four options to choose from for each question), you know you did not do very well. You can honestly say that you did not know the answer to one question; in fact, you could not even eliminate any of the multiple-choice options. When you get your test back, you are pleasantly surprised to see you received a 60%. How could you have thought you did so much worse than you did?

3. Name three activities that are typically learned implicitly.

Discussion Question

1. In a complex implicit-learning task, sometimes people are better off just paying attention to the task instead of trying to figure out the underlying pattern or structure. Why do you think this is the case?

Prototypes

Minimum time to complete this experiment: 20 minutes

Background

Part of cognitive psychology explores the concept of *concepts*. What cognitive events happen when you think about a chair? How is the concept of chair represented in the cognitive system? This is a subtle issue. For example, surely a seat at a formal dining table is chair, but what about a recliner, a stool, a couch, or a tree stump? The issue is important because the representation of concepts is the basis of everything else we can do mentally with concepts. In a very real sense, how we think and what we can learn is largely determined by how we represent concepts.

An efficient way to represent concepts would be to keep only the critical properties of a concept. This set of critical properties is sometimes called a *prototype* or schema. The idea of prototypes is that a person has a mental construct that identifies typical characteristics of various categories. When a person encounters a new object, he/she compares it to the prototypes in memory. If it matches the prototype for a chair well enough, the new object will be classified and treated as a chair. This approach allows new objects to be interpreted on the basis of previously learned information. It is a powerful approach because you do not need to store all previously seen chairs in long-term memory. Instead, only the prototype needs to be kept.

This experiment allows you to participate in a type of experiment that is often used to investigate the creation and storage of concepts. It is a variation of a method used by Posner and Keele (1968), which is one of the earliest studies to systematically explore concept representation in a controlled way. Rather than using an already well-known concept such as a chair, Posner and Keele had participants learn patterns of dots. The patterns were variations of a few prototypes, but the prototypes themselves were not seen during a training phase. During the training phase, participants learned to classify the variations, with the underlying prototype being the basis for correct classifications.

After learning to classify the variants, participants were shown a variety of dot patterns. In particular, they were shown patterns that were shown during the training phase, new variant patterns, and the patterns corresponding to the prototypes. Classification and reaction time performance were nearly equal for the previously seen variants *and* the prototypes. Performance was slightly worse for the new variants. This is significant because both the new variants and the prototypes were never seen during training. To classify dot patterns that were not previously seen, the participants must be using a mental concept of what corresponds to the different categories. Since performance is better for the prototype patterns than for the new variants, the mental concept is similar to the prototype patterns. The conclusion seemed to be that people created a mental representation that was a mixture of the variant patterns used during training (that is, a prototype).

Posner and Keele's experiment led to an intense investigation of concept formation and representation. Much of that research is consistent with prototype theories. However, there are aspects of the experimental data (even in Posner and Keele's experiment) that suggest that the prototype theories cannot be the sole basis for concept representation. For example, our behavior is often influenced by the properties of individual experiences, and some theories of concept formation suggest that this alone can account for the data purported to imply prototypes. Nevertheless, prototypes are a part of many theories of cognition in a variety of forms. This demonstration is a variation of Posner and Keele's experiment.

Instructions

A window will appear that fills nearly the entire screen, and a smaller window will appear with abbreviated instructions. Close the instructions window. You can open it again later from the *CogLab Info.* menu.

Press the *space* bar to start a trial. A fixation point will appear for a second and then will be replaced by randomly placed dots. Your task is to classify the dot pattern as A (press the *z* key) or as B (press the */* key). On the first few trials you will not be able to properly classify the patterns, but you will receive feedback on each trial and so can learn which pattern corresponds to which keypress. You should make your responses as quickly as possible, but try to be accurate.

The experiment consists of separate training and testing phases. The training phase includes at least 60 trials (trials in which a mistake is made are repeated later in the experiment) and the testing phase contains at least 30 trials. Each dot pattern in the training phase is a variation of one of two fixed prototype random dot patterns. The variations are made by randomly taking ten of the twenty-five dots in a prototype and moving them to a new position.

After completing the training phase, a new set of dot patterns is presented. The transition from training to testing is fairly seamless, and you may not notice when it happens. The dot patterns in the testing phase are of six types. One is the prototype that corresponds to the A category. Another is the prototype that corresponds to the B category. The other four patterns are new variations of these prototypes (two variations for each prototype). Each dot pattern is presented five times in random order.

Throughout this experiment your task is always the same. As quickly as possible classify the pattern as A or B. Press the *space* bar to start the next trial.

At the end of the experiment, the experiment window will close and a new window will appear that displays your data as a table and a plot (if appropriate) and provides an explanation of the experiment and results. You can print this information, save it as an html file, or save it in CogLab format. The latter format can be re-opened with CogLab on a CD and by your instructor who may want to combine data from students in your class.

Additional References

Nosofsky, R., & Stanton, R. (2005). Speeded classification in a probabilistic category structure: Contrasting exemplar-retrieval, decision-boundary, and prototype models. *Journal of Experimental Psychology: Human Perception and Performance, 31*, 608-629.

Zaki, S., & Nosofsky, R. (2004). False prototype enhancement effects in dot pattern categorization. *Memory & Cognition, 32*, 390-398.

Smith, J., & Minda, J. (2002). Distinguishing prototype-based and exemplar-based processes in dot-pattern category learning. *Journal of Experimental Psychology: Learning, Memory, and Cognition, 28*, 800-811.

Dopkins, S., & Gleason, T. (1997). Comparing exemplar and prototype models of categorization. *Canadian Journal of Experimental Psychology, 51*, 212-230.

Basic Questions

1. Describe what someone's prototype for a dog might be like.

2. Looking at your experimental results, did you show the prototype effect in this demonstration? How do you know?

3. How does a prototype model explain the prototype effect?

Advanced Questions

1. What is the typicality effect? How does the prototype model account for typicality effects?

2. On a school trip to the zoo, a grade school child sees a penguin and a cardinal for the first time. According to the prototype model, which bird will the child classify as a bird more quickly? Why?

3. You are taking a botany course and you are doing some field work. You come across three trees that you identify as conifer trees. You have seen two of the trees before but not the third. You are surprised because, despite not having seen the third tree before, you identify it as a conifer tree before identifying the other two trees you have seen before. Why might this be the case?

Discussion Question

1. A competing model to the prototype model is the exemplar model. Describe the exemplar model and explain how it accounts for prototype effects.

Monty Hall

Minimum time to complete this experiment: 15 minutes

Background

Most people have a poor understanding of probability. One common problem occurs when evaluating combinations of events. The Monty Hall 3 Door problem is a classic example. Based on the TV game show, Let's Make A Deal, the problem involves 3 doors. Behind one of the doors is a prize. The contestant picks one door. Monty Hall, the eminent emcee, picks one of the remaining two doors to open and shows that the prize is not there. The question is: Do you stay with your original pick or do you change your pick?

You originally begin with a 1 in 3 chance (0.333 probability) of picking the correct door. Many people think that it doesn't matter whether you stay with your original pick or switch after Monty reveals his door.

This interpretation is incorrect. You are better off always switching; over the long term, you will average 66% correct. If you always stay, you will average 33% correct over the long term. If you randomly switch or stay, you will average 50% over the long term.

Here's how to think of it. You pick a door randomly, let's say it is Door 1. You have a 1 out of 3 chance of being correct. This means there is a 2 out of 3 chance that the prize is behind Door 2 or Door 3. If you do nothing, you will be correct approximately 1/3 of the time. However, when Monty Hall shows you that one of the other doors (let's say Door 2) is incorrect, that means that there is now a 2 out of 3 chance that the remaining door is correct. This means that if you pick Door 3, you will be correct approximately 2/3 of the time.

Instructions

An experiment window will appear, and a smaller window will appear with abbreviated instructions. Close the instructions window. You can open it again later from the *CogLab Info.* menu.

This lab simulates the Monty Hall 3 Door Problem. It lets you try out the various options and see how often you would win. Start a trial by clicking on the *Next trial* button. Then select a door. One of the doors will have its contents changed from '?' to '-' to indicate there is no prize. Now, you decide whether to pick your original door again or whether to switch. Once you either confirm your original choice or pick a new door, the winning door will be shown (with a '+') and the other losing door will be shown (with a '-').

To maximize the number of wins, make your first selection randomly and then *always* change to the other door. To minimize the number of wins, make your first selection randomly, then *always* stick with your first choice.

At the end of the experiment, the experiment window will close and a new window will appear that displays your data as a table and a plot (if appropriate) and provides an explanation of the experiment and results. You can print this information, save it as an html file, or save it in CogLab format. The latter format can be re-opened with CogLab on a CD and by your instructor who may want to combine data from students in your class.

Additional References

Burns, B., & Wieth, M. (2004). The collider principle in causal reasoning: Why the Monty Hall dilemma is so hard. *Journal of Experimental Psychology: General, 133*, 434-449.

Tubau, E., & Alonso, D. (2003). Overcoming illusory inferences in a probabilistic counterintuitive problem: The role of explicit representations. *Memory & Cognition, 31*, 596-607.

Krauss, S., & Wang, X. (2003). The psychology of the Monty Hall problem: Discovering psychological mechanisms for solving a tenacious brain teaser. *Journal of Experimental Psychology: General, 132*, 3-22.

Basic Questions

1. For this demonstration, did you try to maximize your wins or maximize your losses? What strategy did you use to accomplish your goal?

2. What is the probability of a coin landing heads up in a fair coin toss? What is the probability of a randomly selected day of the week starting with the letter S?

3. What is the joint probability of rolling a four on a six-sided die and correctly guessing a randomly picked number as being odd or even?

Advanced Questions

1. Imagine a Monty Hall situation with four doors instead of three (there is still only one correct door). After selecting door number one, you are shown that door number two is incorrect. Should you stay with door number one or switch to one of the remaining doors? What are your chances of choosing the right door if you stay with your original door? What are your chances of choosing correctly if you switch?

2. What is the probability of a coin landing heads up on the next coin toss, assuming you had just seen three consecutive coin tosses in which the coin landed heads up?

3. You go to your refrigerator to find something to eat and see three types of leftovers from meals earlier in the week. One of the meals made you sick the last time you ate it but you do not remember which one. You pick one at random and hope for the best. A moment later your roommate comes in and grabs one of the two remaining dishes and indicates that the dish he/she chose was one of the dishes that were okay to eat. At this point, should you stay with your original food choice or switch? Why?

4. If you have a glass jar with five blue marbles, three red marbles, and two green marbles, what is the joint probability of randomly choosing a blue marble (you keep the marble in your hand) and then choosing a red marble?

Discussion Question

1. What is the main difference between an independent event and a dependent event? Give an example of each type of event.

Decision Making

Minimum time to complete this experiment: 10 minutes

Background

Our lives are full of decisions. We must choose what books to read, movies to see, courses to take, person(s) to date, routes to drive, and thousands of other decisions every day. You would hope that people weigh their options carefully and make the best decision possible. Studies in cognitive psychology, however, tell us that the way people make decisions is influenced by a variety of factors. In fact, it is fairly easy to create contexts in which people choose certain options. Many of these tendencies are called "framing effects," because the perceived context or way the choices are "framed" make a big difference, even for situations that are otherwise equivalent. Framing effects have been noted for centuries and many were summarized by Kahneman and Tversky (1982).

This demonstration asks a series of questions. There are two sets of questions. The different sets ask essentially the same questions, but they are presented differently.

Decision-making experiments tend to be done by asking participants to imagine themselves in a particular situation and then to choose between two or more possibilities. This approach depends on the honesty of the participants. You can easily get invalid results by refusing to answer honestly.

Instructions

A window will appear with three buttons and an area that will show the questions. A smaller window will appear with abbreviated instructions. Close the instructions window. You can open it again later from the *CogLab Info.* menu.

On each trial you are given a description of a situation and then two options from which you chose one. Make your choice and then click on the Next trial button to continue.

At the end of the experiment, the experiment window will close and a new window will appear that displays your data as a table and a plot (if appropriate) and provides an explanation of the experiment and results. You can print this information, save it as an html file, or save it in CogLab format. The latter format can be re-opened with CogLab on a CD and by your instructor who may want to combine data from students in your class.

Additional References

Gonzalez, C., Dana, J., Koshino, H., & Just, M. (2005). The framing effect and risky decisions: Examining cognitive functions with fMRI. *Journal of Economic Psychology, 26*, 1-20.

Ronnlund, M., Karlsson, E., Laggnas, E., Larsson, L., & Lindstrom, T. (2005). Risky decision making across three arenas of choice: Are younger and older adults differently susceptible to framing effects? *Journal of General Psychology, 132*, 81-92.

McKenzie, C. (2004). Framing effects in inference tasks--and why they are normatively defensible. *Memory & Cognition, 32*, 874-885.

Levin, I., Johnson, R., Deldin, P., Carstens, L., Cressey, L., & Davis, C. (1986). Framing effects in decisions with completely and incompletely described alternatives. *Organizational Behavior and Human Decision Processes, 38*, 48-64.

Basic Questions

1. What is the main difference between a rational and an irrational decision maker?

2. In relation to decision making, what is a framing effect?

3. Does your individual data show evidence for rational or irrational decision making? Explain your answer.

Advanced Questions

1. Last week you and a friend went to an electronics store. You purchased a television for $600 and your friend bought a video game for $40. Today you saw in the newspaper that the electronics store was having a huge sale and your television is now $580 and your friend's game is $20. You decide it is not worth it for you to go and get a price change, but you call your friend because you can not think of a reason why he/she would not want to go and get a price adjustment. The potential savings for you and your friend is exactly the same so why might you assume your friend would want a price adjustment when you did not?

2. You are a factory manager and, unfortunately, today there was a systems failure. Despite the quick work of your employees, 400 out of the 500 units that your factory produced today were lost. How could you frame the day's productivity (number of units produced) in order to keep up your employees morale?

3. You own a restaurant and decide that all your meals will cost $7 before 5pm and $8 after 5pm. You can advertise this by saying that there will be a discount on meals served before 5pm or you can say there will be a surcharge on meals served after 5pm. How should you advertise your prices? Explain your answer.

Discussion Question

1. Making decisions can be taxing, so people often rely on heuristics. What is a heuristic? Identify and describe one heuristic. Identify a situation when the heuristic you identified would lead you to an erroneous decision.

Risky Decisions

Minimum time to complete this experiment: 10 minutes

Background

Our lives are full of decisions. We must choose what books to read, movies to see, courses to take, person to date, routes to drive, and thousands of other decisions every day. You would hope that people weigh their options carefully and make the best decision possible. Studies in cognitive psychology, however, tell us that the way people make decisions is influenced by a variety of factors. In fact, it is fairly easy to create contexts in which people choose certain options. Many of these tendencies are called "framing effects," because the perceived context or way the choices are "framed" make a big difference, even for situations that are otherwise equivalent. Framing effects have been noted for centuries and many were summarized by Kahneman and Tversky (1982).

To understand some of these framing effects, we need to distinguish between two types of decision-making choices: risky and riskless. A risky choice is one for which there is a probability or chance of different possibilities occurring. For example, if you decide to spend money on a lottery, there is an unknown outcome. You may win a lot of money or you may not. The final outcome is not made by your decision. Your decision simply enters you into a probabilistic situation. A riskless choice is one for which the ultimate outcome is decided by the choice. For example, if you decide to invest your money in a bank account and earn interest, you have made a riskless choice.

Instructions

A window will appear where the experimental questions and choices will be presented, and a smaller window will appear with abbreviated instructions. Close the instructions window. You can open it again later from the *CogLab Info.* menu.

On each trial you will be asked to imagine that you have just received a bonus of a certain amount of money. This amount will vary across questions. You will see two options and you will be asked which one you would prefer. For example, you might see:

Imagine that from your job you get a bonus of $350. You are now faced with a situation where you must choose one of the following options. Which would you choose?

A: A sure loss of $60

 OR

B: 0.4 probability of losing $0 and 0.6 probability of losing $100

If you pick Option A, you will have a final total of $290 because you are guaranteed to lose $60. If you pick Option B, you might lose nothing (and keep all $350) but you might lose $100 and end up with only $250. For this example, if you picked Option B you would lose $100 six times out of ten.

To indicate your preference, click on the button that corresponds to the option that you think is best. If you prefer Option A, click on the A button. If you prefer Option B, click on the B button. In making your decision, try to imagine what the money would actually be worth to you. For example, if you owe a threatening loan shark $290, perhaps it is better to pick the riskless situation (Option A) so that you are certain to be able to completely pay off the debt. On the other hand, if you really need $350, and having $290 will not suffice, perhaps it is better to take the risky option (Option B) and hope you keep all the money. You should make the decision relative to your real-world situation (which is hopefully not so stressful). Some people will like Option A best and some will like Option B best; there are no absolutely correct answers.

Other trials include options with gains instead of losses of money. The starting amount of money, the loss or gain amounts, and the probabilities vary across trials. After you make your choice, click on the Next trial button to start the next trial. There are a total of 12 trials.

At the end of the experiment, the experiment window will close and a new window will appear that displays your data as a table and a plot (if appropriate) and provides an explanation of the experiment and results. You can print this information, save it as an html file, or save it in CogLab format. The latter format can be re-opened with CogLab on a CD and by your instructor who may want to combine data from students in your class.

Additional References

Schlottmann, A., & Tring, J. (2005). How children reason about gains and losses: Framing effects in judgment and choice. *Swiss Journal of Psychology, 64*, 153-171.

Kuhberger, A., Schulte-Mecklenbeck, M., & Perner, J. (1999). The effects of framing, reflection, probability, and payoff on risk preference in choice tasks. *Organizational Behavior and Human Decision Processes, 78*, 204-231.

Kuhberger, A. (1998). The influence of framing on risky decisions: A meta-analysis. *Organizational Behavior and Human Decision Processes, 75*, 23-55

Chien, Y., Lin, C., & Worthley, J. (1996). Effect of framing on adolescents' decision making. *Perceptual and Motor Skills, 83*, 811-819.

Basic Questions

1. What distinguishes a risky choice from a riskless choice?

2. In relation to decision making, what is risk-seeking behavior? When are people likely to be risk-seekers?

3. In relation to decision making, what is risk-avoiding behavior? When are people likely to be risk-avoiders?

Advanced Questions

1. The city council has a difficult decision to make. For the sale of 3 acres of land, a developer has offered them a lump sum of $10,000 or a percentage of the profits from the land development, which they have been told has a 50% chance of being $15,000 and a 50% chance of being $5000. Which option do you think they will choose? Why?

2. Describe a situation (not involving money) in which one would likely be a risk-avoider?

3. For all of the decisions in this demonstration, the expected value for each of the two choice options was equal. Define expected value and explain why it was important for the expected value of the risky choice to be equal to the expected value of the riskless choice.

Discussion Question

1. Identify some factors, not mentioned in this demonstration, that might affect a person's likelihood of engaging in risk-seeking or risk-avoiding behavior. Describe how each of these factors might influence one's behavior.

Typical Reasoning

Minimum time to complete this experiment: 10 minutes

Background

Tversky and Kahneman (1983) are well known for their research showing that people's estimates of probability are often very different from the objective probabilities. The reason, they argue, is that people often use heuristics to help them estimate the answer. Heuristics can be seen as sacrificing some accuracy for an increase in speed. By using heuristics, people can very quickly come up with an answer that is usually good enough for day to day purposes. These heuristics, however, can lead to incorrect judgments.

One of the most striking errors is known as the *conjunction fallacy*. In its most simple form, it says that people think that having both *A* and *B* occur is more likely than having just *A* occur or just *B* occur. According to objective probabilities, the probability of two events occuring has to be less than the probabilities of either of the events happening by themselves. In some circumstances, however, people are more likely to say the conjunction (having both events occur) is more likely.

In particular, the conjunction fallacy is more likely when the items are typical than atypical. For example, read the following:

Julie is 26 years old, has a degree in physical education, has been physically fit since childhood, and loves the outdoors.

People think it is more likely that Julie is a ski instructor who also teaches aerobics (a conjunction involving an activity thought to be more typical of ski instructors) than that Julie is a librarian who also teaches aerobics (a conjunction involving an activity thought to be less typical of librarians). When the activity is particularly typical, the conjunction can be thought more likely than the single events (e.g., that Julie is a ski instructor).

This demonstration is based on an experiment by Shafir, Smith, and Osherson (1990). You will read short descriptions about several people, and you will be asked to rate the probability that these people have certain professions and/or engage in certain activities.

Instructions

An experiment window will appear, and a smaller window will appear with abbreviated instructions. Close the instructions window. You can open it again later from the *CogLab Info.* menu.

Start a trial by clicking once on the "Next trial" button. You will be shown a short description of a person. Read the description carefully. After each description, you will be asked to judge how likely it is, on a scale from 0 to 7, that the person has a particular profession or engages in a particular activity. For example, you might be asked the following:

How likely is it that Bob bets on horse racing?

If you are absolutely certain, based on the description of him that you have just read, that Bob would never bet on horse racing, click on the "0 = Impossible" button. If you are absolutely certain that Bob bets on horse racing, click on the "7 = Certain" button.

There are no correct or incorrect answers. Please respond based on the assumption that the person described is a real person. There are only 12 trials, so please read each description carefully before responding.

At the end of the experiment, the experiment window will close and a new window will appear that displays your data as a table and a plot (if appropriate) and provides an explanation of the experiment and results. You can print this information, save it as an html file, or save it in CogLab format. The latter format can be re-opened with CogLab on a CD and by your instructor who may want to combine data from students in your class.

Additional References

Fisk, J., & Slattery, R. (2005). Reasoning about conjunctive probabilistic concepts in childhood. *Canadian Journal of Experimental Psychology, 59*, 168-178.

Fisk, J., & Pidgeon, N. (1998). Conditional probabilities, potential surprise, and the conjunction fallacy. *Quarterly Journal of Experimental Psychology A: Human Experimental Psychology, 51*, 655-681.

Fantino, E., Kulik, J., Stolarz-Fantino, S., & Wright, W. (1997). The conjunction fallacy: A test of averaging hypotheses. *Psychonomic Bulletin & Review, 4*, 96-101.

Basic Questions

1. What is an advantage of using heuristics? What is a disadvantage of using heuristics?

2. Describe the conjunction fallacy.

3. For this demonstration, on average did you give higher ratings for single events or conjunctions of events? Based on your data from this demonstration, did you make judgments by using objective probabilities? Why or why not?

Advanced Questions

1. You and two of your co-workers have just interviewed a candidate for a job opening at your law firm. Your boss asks you what inferences you drew about the job candidate

during the interview. What can you do to maximize your likelihood of making a correct inference?

2. John is a young, energetic, muscular, and outgoing individual. Estimate the likelihood that he a) is tall and likes sports. and b) is tall, likes sports, and has lots of friends.

3. You and a friend are taking a walk. While on your walk, you pass a middle-aged woman. You tell your friend that she seems like someone who is very intelligent. Your friend agrees but adds that she seems to be very confident as well. Who is more likely to be correct? Why?

Discussion Question

1. What is a stereotype? How do stereotypes relate to the findings of this demonstration?

Wason Selection

Minimum time to complete this experiment: 10 minutes

Background

Research has shown that people find it very difficult to decide what information is necessary in order to test the truth of an abstract logical-reasoning problem. The Wason Selection Task is often used to examine this issue.

A typical experiment using the Wason Selection Task will present some rule, and ask subjects to see if the rule is being violated. Consider the rule: *If a card has a D on one side, it has a 3 on the other side.* Subjects are aware that on the particular set of cards, each one has a letter on one side and a number on the other side. Four cards are shown, such as those below:

Very few people can correctly pick the two cards to turn over to verify the rule. The correct cards are D and 7; most likely, you picked D and 3. Seeing what is on the reverse of the 7 card can lead to falsifying the rule if a D shows up. Seeing what is on the reverse of the 3 card cannot falsify the rule. It can confirm the rule, but not falsify it.

Consider another rule: *If you borrow my car, you must fill up the gas tank.* Four cards are shown below:

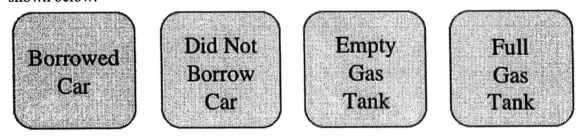

Which cards do you turn over to see if the rule is being followed? You should find that now the answer is more obvious: You want to know what's on the reverse of "borrowed car" and "empty gas tank."

This lab is based on a series of experiments reported by Wason & Shapiro (1971). You will be given a series of rules to verify. Half of them are abstract and half are thematic (the same kind of rule shown above about borrowing a car). The basic idea is that you can test rules when you have some knowledge or experience that is appropriate, but not when you lack this experience. In the thematic case, then, you are not really using logic per se but rather your experience. In the abstract case, you cannot use your experience and have to rely solely on logic.

Instructions

An experiment window will appear, and a smaller window will appear with abbreviated instructions. Close the instructions window. You can open it again later from the *CogLab Info.* menu.

Start a trial by clicking on the *Next trial* button. You will see a rule and four buttons. The rule will ask about two kinds of events. Your task is to select two cards to see what is on the other side so that you can see if the rule is true or false. To select a card, simply click on the appropriate button. Once you have clicked on a card, you cannot change your response.

There are 6 trials, 3 with abstract and 3 with thematic rules.

At the end of the experiment, the experiment window will close and a new window will appear that displays your data as a table and a plot (if appropriate) and provides an explanation of the experiment and results. You can print this information, save it as an html file, or save it in CogLab format. The latter format can be re-opened with CogLab on a CD and by your instructor who may want to combine data from students in your class.

Additional References

Wada, K., & Nittono, H. (2004). Cancel and rethink in the Wason selection task: Further evidence for the heuristic-analytic dual process theory. *Perceptual and Motor Skills, 98*, 1315-1325.

Almor, A., & Sloman, S. (2000). Reasoning versus text processing in the Wason selection task: A nondeontic perspective on perspective effects. *Memory & Cognition, 28*, 1060-1070.

Oaksford, M., & Chater, N. (1995). Information gain explains relevance which explains the selection task. *Cognition, 57*, 97-108.

Sperber, D., Cara, F., & Girotto, V. (1995). Relevance theory explains the selection task. *Cognition, 57*, 31-95.

Basic Questions

1. What are subjects asked to do in a typical Wason Selection Task?

2. Give an example of an abstract rule. Give an example of a thematic rule.

3. Why do participants typically perform better with thematic rules as opposed to abstract rules?

Advanced Questions

1. You and your family have just finished Thanksgiving dinner and some of your family members are starting to get sick. Your sister thinks that the Jello salad is what made everyone sick. During dinner, you noticed that your brother ate some of the Jello salad but your aunt did not. You also know that your grandpa got sick, but your mother did not. Which two people should you talk with to test your sister's hypothesis and what do you need to ask them?

2. Logic can be broken down into deductive reasoning and inductive reasoning. Give an example of each type of reasoning.

3. You have an instructor who told your class that anyone who did not have perfect attendance could not receive an A in the course. At the end of the semester, you want to know if your instructor stuck with this attendance policy. You have a friend who was also in the class and he/she received a B. Would it be helpful to find out if your friend had perfect attendance or not? Explain your answer.

Discussion Question

1. Using what you have learned from this demonstration, what advice would you give a student who is struggling with the concepts being used in his/her algebra class?

GLOSSARY

ABSOLUTE IDENTIFICATION helps to explain why it is difficult to identify objects when they differ from other objects to be identified by only one dimension (for example, length). Identification improves if the items vary by more than one dimension.

APPARENT MOTION The perceived motion of a single light that results when stationary lights are flashed on and off in rapid succession.

ATTENTION The ability to selectively choose some stimuli for processing and ignore others.

ATTENTIONAL BLINK The brief time after paying attention to a stimulus during which attention cannot be focused on a subsequent stimulus.

AUTOMATIZED BEHAVIOR A behavior that proceeds without conscious direction once the series of movements is initiated.

BLIND SPOT The functionally blind area in each eye, located at the optic disk. If light falls on this area, we can't see it.

BRAIN ASYMMETRY The two distinct hemispheres of the brain have different capabilities. The left hemisphere is said to deal with language and analytical thought, while the right hemisphere is said to deal with spatial relations and creativity.

BROWN-PETERSON EFFECT showed that there is a separate short-term memory (STM) system that holds information for several seconds. Without an active effort by the participant, information in STM fades away.

C is a measure of response bias in a signal-detection experiment; a value greater than zero indicates a conservative bias and a value less than zero indicates a liberal bias.

CATEGORICAL PERCEPTION-DISCRIMINATION refers to the ability to detect whether two stimuli are the same or different.

CATEGORICAL PERCEPTION-IDENTIFICATION refers to the point at which one's categorical perception changes from one distinct category to another.

CHANGE BLINDNESS it is the inability to detect changes in the environment or on a cognitive task.

CHANGE DETECTION it is the ability to detect changes in the environment or on a cognitive task.

CLASSICAL CONDITIONING is a type of learning in which a stimulus acquires the capacity to stimulate a response that was originally brought about by another stimulus, that is, learning by association.

CONJUNCTIVE SEARCH is the type of search performed in a visual-search task when identifying the target requires distinguishing it from distractors on more than one dimension.

CORRECT REJECTION is a trial in a signal-detection experiment in which a participant correctly reports that a target was not present.

DISTRACTOR TASK is a task (such as mental arithmetic) designed to prevent active rehearsal of information in short-term memory.

D-prime (d′) is a measure of participant sensitivity in a signal detection experiment; the larger the d′ the greater the sensitivity.

ENCODING SPECIFICITY The memory of an event is related to the interaction between the properties of the encoded event and the properties of the encoded retrieval information.

ENDOGENEOUS CUE is a cue that must be identified and intentionally acted upon by the participant.

EXHAUSTIVE SEARCH is a search of memory that ends only after all items have been accessed.

EXOGENOUS CUE is a cue that automatically draws one's attention to the location of its presentation.

EXPLICIT LEARNING occurs when one consciously or intentionally acquires knowledge about a stimulus or a task.

FALSE ALARM is a trial in a signal-detection experiment in which a participant incorrectly reports that a target is present.

FALSE MEMORY is a memory that a person recalls about things that did not occur. It is seen in therapeutic settings.

FORGOT-IT-ALL-ALONG is a memory phenomenon in which an individual experiences an event, correctly recalls the event when tested, but later forgets that they accurately remembered the event during the recall test.

FOVEA is the central area on the retina of each eye that is densely packed with light sensitive receptors. We turn our fovea toward whatever we are looking at to see the details of that object better.

FRAMING EFFECTS refer to the influence of context on the way people make decisions.

GARNER TASK The Garner task is a speeded classification test of the influence of irrelevant information on a perceptual task.

GARNER TASK – INTEGRAL When dimensions in a Garner task are integral, they are often processed as one dimension and interference occurs, hence processing speeds decrease. One example is hue and brightness.

GARNER TASK – SEPARABLE When dimensions in a Garner task are separable, they are often processed as separate dimensions and there is no interference effect. One example is hue and size.

GESTALT PSYCHOLOGY is an area of psychology that follows the premise that people organize their perceptions according to certain patterns, so that what you see as a whole is not equal to the sum of its parts.

HEURISTICS are quickly produced problem solving short cuts that may not always lead to a correct answer.

HIT is a trial in a signal-detection experiment in which a participant correctly identifies a target.

ICONIC STORE is a visual sensory storage system lasting a few hundred milliseconds.

IMPLICIT LEARNING occurs when one unconsciously or unintentionally acquires knowledge about a stimulus or a task.

INTERSTIMULUS INTERVAL (ISI) is the period of time between the offset of a first stimulus and the onset of a second stimulus.

IRRELEVANT SPEECH EFFECT The memory for a list of items may be impaired when an irrelevant speech (auditory) stimulus follows the presentation of the list, even when the list is visually presented.

KORTE'S LAWS are statements describing aspects of apparent motion, such as the relation between the ISI and the spatial separation required for motion to be perceived.

LEVELS OF PROCESSING In general, memory is better when it is processed at a deep level compared to a shallow level. Structural decisions are shallow, while semantics require deeper processing.

LEXICAL DECISION is a test of the mental lexicon.

LEXICON is a mental dictionary containing information about a word's meaning, its part of language, and its relationship to other words.

LINK WORD is a mnemonic technique that uses interactive imagery to associate a familiar word with a novel or new word. It is often used to learn a new language.

Log(alpha) is a measure of participant sensitivity in a signal-detection experiment.

MASKING is the impaired performance on the judgment of a target stimulus due to the presentation of another stimulus (the mask).

MEMORY SPAN is the capacity of short-term or working memory. It is measured in how many list items a participant can recall in their correct order.

MENTAL ROTATION is a technique used to study the nature of mental images. The greater the degree of rotation, the slower the reaction-time.

MENTAL SCANNING is the active process of exploring cognitive representations.

METACONSTRAST MASKING is a special case of masking in which the target and mask have no overlapping contours and the mask is presented after the target.

METHOD OF CONSTANT STIMULI is a psychophysical method that requires the observer to make judgments about stimuli in terms of whether they are perceived to be greater or less than a standard stimulus.

MISS is a trial in a signal-detection experiment in which a participant fails to detect a target.

MNEMONIC DEVICE is a technique used to increase one's memory.

MODALITY EFFECTS can help to explain why the memory for the last item in a list of items improves when it is presented in specific modalities, for example when a list is read out loud or is silently mouthed.

MONTY HALL is a classic problem of understanding probability. You are given 3 choices to pick from and only one of these choices is correct. After making your selection, you are shown that 1 of the 2 remaining choices was incorrect. You are then asked if you wish to stay with your original choice or switch to the remaining choice. According to the Monty Hall logic, you increase your probability of winning over the long term if you always switch. Probability increases from 1/3 (0.33) to 2/3 (0.66).

MULLER-LYER ILLUSION is the arrow illusion in which the shank with the outward wings appears longer than the shank with the inward wings even though the shanks are the same objective length.

OPERATION SPAN refers to the number of sequential operation-word strings that a participant can attend to. The greater your operation span, the greater the attention span.

OPTIC DISK is the region in each eye where the optic nerve exits; it contains no light-sensitive receptors and produces the blind spot.

PARALLEL SEARCH is a search of memory in which every item is accessed simultaneously.

PARTIAL REPORT is the technique George Sperling used in his early studies of the sensory memory. It is called partial because participants were asked to recall only one row of the presented matrices. (Also see whole report.)

PERCEPTUAL SPAN is the amount of information that can be gathered in a single precept.

PHONOLOGICAL SIMILARITY Performance tends to decrease when the items of a list sound similar than when the items sound different.

POSITION ERROR GRADIENTS help to explain the systematic errors that an individual may make when recalling a list of items. Generally, adjacent items are mixed up.

PRIMACY EFFECT The first few items in a list are remembered particularly well in a free recall task.

PROTOTYPE is a mental construct that has the critical properties of a concept. It is used to identify new objects.

PSYCHOMETRIC FUNCTION is a graph that relates the probability of a certain response to variations in a physical characteristic of a stimulus.

PSYCHOPHYSICS is a sub-discipline of psychology that attempts to relate reported characteristics of perception to physical properties of stimuli that give rise to those reports.

RECENCY EFFECT The last few items in a list are remembered particularly well in a free recall task.

RECEPTIVE FIELD is any stimulus that changes a neuron's firing rate.

REMEMBER/KNOW is a recognition memory phenomenon that tries to distinguish between memories that one *remembers*, consciously aware of some aspect of the original learning situation, or *knows*, having no conscious awareness of the learning situation.

RISKY DECISIONS In decision-making, the choice of taking a risk or not taking a risk is strongly influenced by how the situation is framed. A risky choice is one in which there is a probability or chance of different possibilities occurring. A riskless choice is one in which the ultimate outcome is decided by the choice.

SELF-REFERENT EXAMPLES are examples that are personally relevant. They tend to improve one's memory.

SELF-TERMINATING SEARCH is a search of memory that ends as soon as a match has been found.

SERIAL POSITION Memory of an item depends on where it is positioned within a list. The items at the beginning and the end tend to be remembered more often than the items in the middle. (Also see recency and primacy effects.)

SERIAL SEARCH is a search of memory in which items are accessed successively.

SIGNAL DETECTION is a procedure that provides a separate measure of sensitivity and response bias for situations in which observers are required to detect the presence of a faint target.

SIGNAL-DETECTION THEORY proposes that the detection of a stimulus involves sensory processes as well as decision processes.

SIMON EFFECT Response time may be reduced and accuracy may increase when a stimulus is presented in the same relative location as the response required.

SPATIAL CUEING A participant's responses may be faster at locating a target that is previously cued but slower when the target's location is not previously cued.

STERNBERG SEARCH Saul Sternberg developed this technique of exploring how information is retrieved from short-term memory.

STROOP EFFECT refers to the difficulty participants have in naming ink colors of color words when the ink colors and the color words do not agree.

SUFFIX EFFECT The recall of the last item in a list that is read aloud may be impaired if the list is followed by an irrelevant suffix.

TYPICAL REASONING When estimating likelihoods, individuals tend to make reasoning errors based on time-saving heuristics and generalizations. One reasoning error we make is the *conjunction fallacy*, in which two typical events seem more probable that one typical event.

VISUAL SCOTOMA is a damaged part of the retina that causes a blind spot.

VISUAL SEARCH is a task in which the participant searches a visual image for the presence of a particular item. The participant responds as quickly as possible once the item is found or once he/she is certain that the item is not present.

VON RESTORFF EFFECT is a recall-memory phenomenon that helps to explain why the memory of an item in a list improves if it is distinctive from the surrounding items.

WASON SELECTION TASK is a task that is used to test the truth of an abstract logical rule. Four cards with information on both sides are displayed and participants are asked which 2 cards must be turned over in order to verify the given rule.

WHOLE REPORT Early memory studies used this technique in which participants recall a whole matrix of letters. This technique showed a recall ability of 4.5 items.

WORD SUPERIORITY A letter that is part of a word is recognized more easily than a letter in isolation.